THE CONQUEROR'S NERVE

Dr. Nonye Okoye

To request permission, contact +2348033233734
or nonyeokoyecounselling@gmail.com

First Edition: August, 2024

ISBN: 978-978-796-809-3

Printed in Nigeria

Preface

*Take heed now; for the Lord hath chosen thee to build an house for the sanctuary: **be strong, and do it**. And David said to Solomon his son, **Be strong and of good courage, and do it**: fear not, nor be dismayed: for the Lord God, even my God, will be with thee; he will not fail thee, nor forsake thee, until thou hast finished all the work for the service of the house of the Lord* (1 Chr. 28:10, 20).

Life is full of struggles, and very often, we think prayer is the sole solution. Prayer is powerful and extremely important, but inaction makes it ineffective. King David was a prayer warrior, yet he repeatedly encouraged his son, Solomon, to be strong and to build the sanctuary God appointed him to build. Being a man of prayer and action, he knew that without determination, the project would only remain in his son's imagination, even though everything needed for the building was available, including God's presence (1 Chronicles 22:5). Every person in this world has some work to do. Whatever it is, strength of heart and personal commitment are required to get it done.

There are a few unforgettable experiences I had at ages eight, twelve, and fourteen, respectively. Two of these happened when I was eight years old. Both were fights between me and a couple of my classmates, on different occasions. Both of them (a boy and a girl) were confident about defeating me in a fight, so they each played several pranks on me to force a violent response from me, which they hoped would eventually result in a fight.

I did all I could to avoid their shenanigans. One fateful day, the girl blocked my path during our exercise runs in school. We both hit the ground and sustained injuries. She instantly blamed me for the mishap and vowed to deal with me once the school day was over. True to her word, she accosted me and stood in my way after school. As expected, a fight broke out between us. Guess what? I beat her black and blue!

Her mother had to accompany her to report the situation to my sister, who was my guardian. My sister was objective in her judgment, and refused to beat me, stating that the girl was older than me, and her mother was wrong for defending her actions. The girl learned a lesson that day and started trying to get in my good books.

That wasn't the end of my troubles, however. As for the boy, his turn came one day when he blocked my way after school and tried to stop me from leaving the classroom. We fought, and yes, I beat him too! We somehow moved from the classroom to the school compound, where I threw him down and sat on him in front of his friends, who were initially hailing him. He felt very ashamed and after that day, he became my silent admirer.

When I was twelve, a boy from a neighboring village joined my class. His mother was a teacher in my school, which meant special privileges. He was untouchable, and he and his cousins were part of a gang feared by many children. One evening, I went to that village to greet my aunt and found the boy and other members of that unruly gang in front of my aunt's compound. He began several antics to instigate a fight with me. He succeeded, but as usual, the tables turned against him. His cousins didn't join in the fight and I didn't hesitate to teach him a lesson. After the fight, he stayed as far away from me as possible, but I gained his cousins' respect.

Last but not least, this experience occurred when I was fourteen, in a girls-only secondary school. I was walking home from school one day when my classmate started making jokes about my appearance. It was obvious she was trying to incite a brawl, but I didn't give her the satisfaction, especially since I'd done nothing to offend her. At some point, I wanted to call her 'Shot put', seeing she was shorter than me. But I restrained myself, knowing she had no control over her height, and my insult would be direct to God, her Creator. I kept walking and after a while, I remembered a word I'd learned from the dictionary a short while back. I turned to her and said, "You see, I don't exchange words with riffraff like you."

Laughter rippled through the crowd of students who were watching, and they taunted my *opponent*, saying she shouldn't give a comeback till she defined the word. She couldn't, and the battle ended there. The students hailed me for my vocabulary and made fun of her till we parted ways.

Those experiences left an indelible mark on my mind. I continue to learn from them. As I reminisce, I wonder how I got the courage, strength, and wisdom to face those fights and emerge the winner. I've realized that God is ever ready to help me overcome when I refuse to be an onlooker in my own affairs and choose to rise up to do what only I can do. Christianity doesn't guarantee trouble-free life, but we're sure of victory even in the hard times. Talking is the easiest thing in the world. If that alone achieves success, no one can be a failure.

Unless you hold yourself responsible for your progress, you will always cower from threats and oppositions and spend your days dreaming about what can be. Dreams or prophecies, however good or big, do not guarantee success. Threats and challenges precede victory, so the bigger the dreams or prophecies concerning you, the more troubles you face to accomplish them.

Perseverance is the price for success!

I hope you will receive freedom from whatever traps you and abundantly blessed as you read through this book.

Nonye Okoye, PhD
August 2024
+2348033233734, Lagos
nonyeokoyecounselling@gmail.com

This page is intentionally left blank

Dedication

I dedicate this book to everyone who wants to witness the glory of God all over the world, and to the memories of my beloved mother, Ezinne Priscilla Nwoyibo Obi, sister-in-law, Chiebonem Florence Obi, and brother, Obed Chukwuemeka Obi who would have been so much excited at the publication of this book.

This page is intentionally left blank

Acknowledgement

Nothing is possible without God. I am therefore indebted to the Almighty God, the King of kings and the Lord of lords, the Giver of life and experience, who made the production of this book a reality.

Success is not realizable without the help of significant others; hence, I will not fail to recognize some people whom the Lord at one point or the other used to mold me since I was born. I appreciate my late mother, Ezinne Priscilla Nwoyibo Obi (1933-2015), and my late father, Enoch Nwankwo Obi, who left this world forty-three years before my mother. My mama was my confidante right from childhood, and I learned from her how to avoid bickering while being accommodating.

I'm grateful to my mother-in-law, Mrs. Mgboye Okoye (AKA Gold), for her love. She tolerates my weaknesses and cares for my well-being. Back when my mother was alive, both women showed me love without measure. Now that my mother is gone, my mother-in-law still keeps the love channel open. What a great blessing to have had two selfless mothers. A sweet experience indeed.

I cannot overlook the kindness and support of my brothers (the Obis)–Sunday Sydney, Ken Ikechukwu, and late Obed Chukwuemeka (1961-2023)–and their wives, Cecilia, late Florence Chiebonem (1974-2019), and Philomina Chinwe respectively, and my only sister, Mrs. Irene Agụ. Senior bros and sis, you've never stopped being compassionate towards me, your little sis, nor did you abandon me while I tried to find my footing at every stage of life. I feel highly honored to have stayed in the same womb as you, and I'm grateful for all the comfort you've been providing me since I was born. Only God can reward you enough; any human reward will be too little to count.

I feel a deep sense of gratitude to my cousin, Fred Obi, and his wife, Chinyere. God, who never ignores good deeds, will reward you beyond measure. I appreciate the support of my brothers-in-law (the Okoyes)–Okechukwu Richard, Ozoemena Israel, Obidike Simon–and their wives respectively–Obiageli, Adaora, and Amaka–who I see not just as marriage mates but as sisters and friends. My special thanks to Obiageli Okoye (Mrs.) LLB, FICMC, for her immense contribution to the progress of this work.

I appreciate the benevolence of the late Joe Ụwaechina, a onetime lecturer at the Federal Polytechnic Oko, Anambra State, who sacrificed time to share Scriptures with me when I was a baby Christian. I am thankful to Mrs Chinwe Madichie for her invaluable support. I acknowledge my PhD supervisors: Professor Ngozi N. Osarenren and Professor Mopeola

O. Omoegun, of the Department of Educational Foundation, University of Lagos, whose constructive criticisms and encouragements helped me navigate through the years of PhD-in-view.

I am grateful to my son, Chidubem Okoye, Esq., who began the typing of this manuscript; and my daughters, Chisom Okoye, for her technical support, and Chekwube Okoye, who took pains to read through the manuscript. I cannot by whatever means appreciate enough the sacrifices and encouragements of the rest of my precious children and beloved husband, Sam Okoye, from the beginning to the publishing of this book. You all are helpful and inspiring; indeed, you are assets from the Most High God. I trust God to keep us knit together, walking in unity for greater feats.

I appreciate all my brethren in the Lord, relatives, family friends, and well-wishers, who are too many to mention. May God's favor be your daily experience.

I recognize all God-fearing people and the members of the body of Christ worldwide on whose behalf God directed me to write this book. I'm thankful to God for the opportunity to serve you. I love you all.

May we all remain humble and teachable in the hands of the Holy Spirit so we can fulfill the purpose of our creation in the name of Jesus Christ. Amen.

Nonye Okoye, PhD

Contents

Chapter One

FAITH

God is a Spirit: and they that worship him must worship him in spirit and in truth (John 4:24).

L ife has its foothold in the spirit. Whatever we see on the earth's surface reflects what goes on in the spirit world. Everything that happens to us first occurs in the spirit. We cannot decisively do anything or truly solve problems if we do not operate from the spirit.

The spiritual world holds the physical.

Faith is the only genuine way to connect our spirits to the spirit realm and have personal and unbroken fellowship with the Spirit of God. **Genuine worship of God is a spiritual activity with the inevitable substance of truth.** God is a Spirit and has direct contact with the spirit of man. He does not directly relate to the soul or the body of man.

But there is a spirit in man: and the inspiration of the Almighty giveth them understanding (Job 32:8). The spirit of man is the candle of the LORD, searching all the inward parts of the belly (Proverbs 20:27).

Nothing pleases God like unwavering faith in His being and His promises. God considered Abraham righteous because of his firm belief in Him, not because of his good works or personal morality (Gen. 15:6, Rom. 4:2-3). *But **without faith** it is **impossible** to please Him, for he who comes to God must believe that He is, and that He is a rewarder of those who **diligently** seek Him* (Heb. 11:6).

Faith is about confidence in God in all situations, whether His promises are fulfilled or still pending. Our personal faith in Christ *(not in other entities or ourselves)* gives us access to the throne of God (John 14:6, Heb.4:14-16).

Faith can either be **alive (and active)** or **dead (and dormant)**. God's Word builds and sustains active faith (Rom. 10:17). Hence active faith carries God's mobile presence and dynamic power, demonstrating His omnipresence, omniscience, and omnipotence. Dormant faith is prone to unbelief, causing one to doubt God's goodness and hindering miracles (Matt. 13:58). It creates a misconception of God and spreads fear, error, and falsehood.

Fear torments and paralyzes man (1 John 4:18b, Heb. 2:15), but active faith combats it. We know there is more to life than meets the eye, and the only way you overcome life's battles as they unfold is to have a personal, active faith in God (Hab. 2:4b).

The Scripture is replete with instructions that inspire one to choose faith over fear. Consider the following verses.

Thus says the LORD to you: Do not be afraid nor dismayed ... for the battle is not yours, but God's (2 Chr. 20:15). *Do not be afraid.* **Stand still**, *and see the salvation of the LORD ... The LORD will fight for you, and you shall hold your peace* (Ex. 14:13-14). *Be not afraid, only believe* (Mark 5:36). **Be still**, *and know that I am God: I will be exalted among the heathen, I will be exalted in the earth* (Ps. 46:10).

God is not man; all He requires of you is confidence in Him so He can defend you. Everything we need for life on earth already exists in *God, who quickeneth the dead, and calleth those things which be not as though they were* (Rom. 4:17).

Faith is not motivation, but an attitude of the heart; faith is in us. God gave every man a measure of faith (Rom. 12:3), enough at least to believe in His existence and power (Rom. 1:20).

Now faith is the substance of things hoped for, the evidence of things not seen (Heb. 11:1). Faith is the conviction that your expectation is fulfilled, even though at the moment, you may have no physical evidence to prove it. It is seeing with the eye of your spirit the

> **Faith gives God the center stage and applauds Him from the gallery.**

reality of God's promises, despite the contradictory picture this material world presents.

Faith implies Hope and the two work together. Faith deals with the present, and looks to the Promisor who is ever faithful, while Hope deals with the future and waits on the promise which is certain. Hope strengthens faith until she receives the promise. However, hope is fantasy, where there is no active faith and will eventually receive nothing.

Faith does not deny a problem or a particular condition, but settles on God's will concerning it. It does not fix her eyes on the nagging conditions of life but on God, who is above them; therefore, it stands on God's Word to counter anything that opposes the promise or counsel of God.

For instance, when Jesus got the news of Lazarus' sickness, He said the sickness would not end in death but in the glory of God. Yet Lazarus died. Jesus made light of the news of Lazarus' death and was not in a haste to visit and pray for him. He told His disciples that Lazarus was sleeping, and He was going to wake him up. He indeed called him back to life after four days of being in the grave. Here, the death was against the promise of God, so Jesus reverted it (John 11:1-6, 11-15, 33- 34, 39, 43-44). It is obvious from Ezekiel (13:18-23) that witchcraft can cut short someone's life. For this reason, Jesus gave His disciples power to raise the dead and deal with untimely death (Matt. 10:8).

Again, if you are experiencing financial difficulties, Faith does not dismiss the fact that you presently eat from hand to mouth or lack money for personal expenses but says, **'I do not accommodate penury, for Jesus has paid the price of poverty for me; therefore, I am rich and not poor; a giver and not a beggar'** (2 Cor. 8:9; Deut. 28:12; Ps.113:7-8). In the instance of delayed childbearing, Faith says, **'I disagree with everything that hinders my womb from conception; I'm a child of God and shall not be barren'** (Ex. 23:26; Ps.113:9).

The extent we realize the promises of God depends on the proportion of our faith. Faith believes **and** speaks (2 Cor. 4:13). Declare the promises of God over whatever situation you find yourself in if you truly believe His Word.

The psalmist spoke health into existence when he was deadly sick because he believed the sickness would not shorten his life. *The sorrows of death compassed me, and the pains of hell gat hold upon me: I found trouble and sorrow. I will walk before the LORD in the land of the living. I believe, therefore have I spoken: I was greatly afflicted* (Ps. 116:3, 9-10).

> **Your action reveals your conviction.**

Creative and destructive power lies in your tongue and you are ultimately what you say (Prov. 18:21). You will have joy and peace and be full of hope if you do not doubt God's promises (Rom. 15:13), but you will worry if you are in doubt.

Faith is not baseless belief–it usually accompanies knowledge. *So then faith comes by hearing, and hearing by the word of God* (Rom. 10:17). The Christian faith feeds on the knowledge of the grace and character of God, and relies on God's power for victory (1 John 5:4; cf. 1 Tim. 6:12; 2 Cor. 10:3-5). *... what shall I... say... of Gedeon... Barak... who through faith subdued kingdoms, wrought righteousness, obtained promises, stopped the mouth of lions* (Heb. 11:32-33).

God is His word and does not fail (John 1:1; Num. 23:19; Matt. 5:18), but unbelief robs us of His promises. Our faith fails when we lose hope in God's Word (cf. Luke 22:32); hope keeps faith alive till God's visitation.

*... but the word preached did not profit them, **not being mixed with faith**... (Heb. 4:2).*

*... all things are possible to him that **believeth** (Mark 9:23).*

We have to live in hope to enjoy the salvation we received through faith. People lose hope when they reject the comfort of the Scriptures (Rom. 15:4) and take solace in the words of men. They eventually fall victim to deceit and unbelief. If you belittle God and doubt His ability to change the course of any event for your good, you exalt the devil and inadvertently believe the situation will turn out worse.

Ten out of the twelve spies to the land of Canaan undermined God's power and exaggerated the might of the enemy in their report, causing unbelief in the people's hearts and turning their eleven-day journey into a great curse of forty years wandering and death (Num. 13:28-29; 14:1, 33-34; cf. Deut. 1:2). Having believed the lies, the congregation rejected the account of the two spies who were full of faith and wanted immediate action for the possession of the Promised Land.

Then Caleb stilled the people before Moses, and said, Let us go up at once and possess it; for we can well overcome it. But the men that went up with him said, We be not able to go up against the people; for they are stronger than we. And they brought up an evil report of the land which they had searched unto the children of Israel, saying, The land, through which we have gone to search it, is a land that eateth up the inhabitants thereof; and all the people that we saw in it are men of great stature. And there we saw the giants, the sons of Anak, which come of the giants: and we were in our own sight as grasshoppers, and so we were in their sight (Num. 13:30-33; cf. 14:6-10).

Faithlessness is self-bewitchment, and it is contagious. **Be careful who you listen to and what manner of information you take in**. People often make up stories to mask their lack of trust in God, rather than accept they have a problem of unbelief. The spies carried out their investigation secretly, so how could they have known the mind of the giants towards them–how did they get the information from the giants? What made their report engender unrest in the community? Can fear operate when faith is alive?

Faith does not deny feelings, but undeterred by their restrictions and bondage and forges ahead. Feelings fluctuate and agree with faith when things are smooth, but often hold back when things are rough.

> *Apply faith in your daily living and watch all things turn around for your good.*

The book of Habakkuk, for example, opens with the prophet Habakkuk's emotional state of confusion, fear, doubt, and sadness, because of the troubles in his nation, Israel (Hab. 1:1-4). However, it ends with his personal decision to trust God and rejoice in the hope of His salvation despite the momentary chaos in the land (Hab. 3:17-19).

Do not lose hope whenever your desire is unfulfilled, even though you manifested faith. The Omniscient God honors our faith in diverse ways, sometimes in the opposite direction. But be rest assured, He has your best interest at heart and will make all things work for your good. The most important thing is that you hold on to your faith in total obedience to the very end of any matter. The abiding presence of God in your life is proof that everything is culminating in God's perfect will, which is best for you. Therefore, let **faith overrule feelings.**

Chapter Two

FORGIVENESS

And whenever you stand praying, if you have anything against anyone,
forgive him, that your Father in heaven may also forgive you your trespasses
(Mark 11:25).

Every experience whether negative or positive, is part of the Christian training that culminates in us achieving our divine purpose. It is natural to be angry with people who hurt us, or in unpleasant circumstances. However, our disposition will be different if we see both the people and the situations as role players in our divine destiny. Instead of being angry towards His persecutors or situations, our Lord Jesus seized those opportunities to exemplify forgiveness, knowing they were playing their respective roles in the track of events predetermined for Him by God; His Father and our Father (John 20:17b).

None of the things that happened at distinct stages of Jesus' life were by chance (cf. Ps. 139:16). When His hour of trial was at hand, He said, *The Son of Man indeed goes just as it is **written** of Him...* (Mark 14:21). At His arrest, He rebuked Peter for cutting off the ear of the high priest's servant in His defense and stressed that the occasion was as designed by God (Matt. 26:52-56). On the cross, He prayed for the Forgiveness of His persecutors–*Then said Jesus, Father, forgive them; for they know not what they do...* (Luke 23:34).

> **Life is in stages and every experience counts.**

Jesus said offense is inevitable in this world (Luke 17:1). Hence, He provides forgiveness as the drug to treat hurt. Peter was quick to ask Him the number of times he was to take this drug each day. Jesus' answer reveals that the forgiveness drug has no harmful side effects and no risk of overdose or abuse. Therefore, take it as much as 490 times a day!

Then Peter came to Him and said, "Lord, how often shall my brother sin against me, and I forgive him? Up to seven times?" Jesus says to him, "I *do not say to you, up to seven times, but up to **seventy times seven**"* (Matt. 18:21-22). In effect, Jesus is saying there is no limit to forgiveness as a particular person cannot offend you up to 490 times a day. By this, He teaches us the principle of constant forgiveness–

> **Forgiveness drug/ 490 times daily**

any time you feel hurt, take the forgiveness drug to get your healing.

It is better to take the forgiveness drug in 'injection format' as it enables you to forgive ahead, rather than the 'tablet format' that makes you wait to be offended before deciding to forgive. Take the injection regularly so you will forgive your offenders without their apology and even before they offend you. You receive healing when you forgive others (Ps. 147:3). In addition, you will be true to your confession when you stand before God in prayer and say, *forgive me my debts, as I forgive my debtors* (Matt. 6:12 rephrased).

Your offenders may not always be other people. If you have failed or deceived yourself and the devil tortures you with regret, forgive yourself and cease to be mad at yourself. God has forgiven you, and by the blood of Jesus Christ removed the guilt of sin from you, provided you have genuinely received Christ into your life and turned away from sin (1 John 1:9; cf. Prov. 28:13). Regret will hinder you from enjoying the forgiveness of God and.

Again, if in ignorance you feel bitter about God, let go. Many people are angry with God because they think He has failed them, whereas they fail themselves by their wrong acts. *The foolishness of man perverteth his way: and his heart fretteth against the LORD* (Prov. 19:3).

You hold yourself in bondage and hurt yourself more if you refuse to forgive. People think they will benefit their offenders if they give up grudges against them. If you have malaria and take anti-malarial medication, who gets the healing: you or the mosquito whose bite caused the illness?

> **Healthy mind, healthy body.**

...anger rests in the bosom of fools (Eccl. 7:9). Forgiveness is for your own health and wealth; try it!

Anger eats you up on the inside and overtime shows on the outside, it affects all aspects of you: spirit, soul, and body. Like other negative emotions, it causes mental breakdowns and physical ill-health. Our hearts and bodies have chemical connections, so your thoughts and feelings affect your body. *Heaviness in the heart of man maketh it stoop: but a good word maketh it glad. A sound heart is the life of the flesh: but envy the rottenness of the bones. A merry heart doeth good like medicine: but a broken spirit drieth the bones* (Prov. 12:25; 14:30; 17:22;see also 15:13, 15).

> **Anger step by step ends in depression.**

Anger keeps you on edge and makes it hard for you to relax and think clearly. It prevents you from acting reasonably. If you have anger issues, your foes can always set you up with provocation so that you *re-act* instead of *act*. For instance, if someone screams at you and you scream back, you re-acted in the sense that you did not plan to scream at the person but did so because the person started it. You act when you consider the scream and come up with your own strategy on how to deal with it. You are **in control** of your emotions when you **act**, but subject to **manipulation** when you **re-act**. People's behavior will not determine your responses if you think before you act.

Reacting in anger is a natural and immature way of handling a problem. It does not solve, but multiplies the problem and makes the situation worse. It sets people against each other and saturates the environment with tension and anxiety. *Therefore, cease from anger and forsake wrath, for the wrath of man does not produce the righteousness of God* (Ps. 37:8; James 1:20). *For wrath kills a foolish man, And envy slays a simple one* (Job 5:2).

> **Kill anger or it kills you.**

Whatever you do out of personal hurt focuses on yourself and can neither achieve God's purpose nor secure God's blessings. The anger that draws God's attention and brings restoration is the anger shown against sin: anger in defense of God's reputation, which pacifies His wrath (cf. Numb. 25:6-13; John 2:13-17).

Assignment - Think of any problem(s) you solved with anger, list the gains and losses side by side, and then compare and contrast.

Accumulated anger develops into hatred and eventually murder (1 John 3:15). We can murder with our tongues, not just guns. *Death and life are in the power of the tongue...* (Prov. 18:21). *Then said they, Come, and let us devise devices against Jeremiah ... and let us **smite** him with the **tongue**...* (Jer. 18:18).

Anger destroys opportunities that gentle dispositions would have offered if we had let the Holy Spirit convict the offenders of their wrongdoings (John 16:8). You may ask, 'Can't I be angry when provoked'? Yes, you can. It is your right and natural. But being quick to anger causes you more damage (Ex. 32:19), and retention of anger makes you vulnerable to the devil.

Be not hasty in thy spirit to be angry: for anger resteth in the bosom of fools (Eccl. 7:9). *Be angry, and do not sin: do not let the sun go down on your wrath, nor give place to the devil* (Eph. 4:26-27).

From these verses, we observe that anger can be an immediate natural reaction to an offense, but allowing the anger to linger opens the offended up to demonic attacks (cf. Matt. 18:34). Seeing that anger cannot undo a provocation, it is wise to give room for forgiveness. Provocations are distractions that will obscure your mind and redirect your attention if you fail to overlook them. Forgiveness frees your mind and enables you to see clearly in the spirit. *The discretion of a man makes him slow to anger, And his glory is to overlook a transgression* (Prov. 19:11).

When you forgive someone, you bear no grudge against them. The popular saying 'I forgive but I don't forget' may be a subtle way to justify un-forgiveness. Forgiveness is not memory loss but the release of both the offense and the offender. A negative review of offenses makes one live in perpetual hurt. Forgiving an offender does not mean that you no longer remember the offense, but that memory

> **Forgiveness is not memory loss.**

of the offense no longer hurts you or determines the way you treat the offender.

The feeling of hurt when you remember the experience reveals that there are still unresolved issues about the offender.

Nothing will trigger hurt feeling if you completely forgive the offender and choose to not retaliate. Joseph's brothers were very unkind to him but he gave them a good treat in return, not because he did not remember their wickedness against him but because he held nothing against them, knowing God allowed the events for blessings (Gen. 37:4, 8, 18, 24, 28; 42:8-9; 43:30-31; 45:1-5; 50:15-21).

Again, Moses prayed for Miriam's recovery from leprosy notwithstanding that the leprosy was the consequence of her badmouthing him (Num. 12:1-2, 9-10, 13). If Moses had not forgiven Miriam, he would probably choose to believe she was getting what she deserved, and would not pray for her healing.

We will not find it difficult to forgive our offenders if we have the right perspective of the sovereignty of God. You cannot have God as sovereign and still leave things to *luck, chance, or fate.* These three words give the impression that things occur haphazardly. It means no one is in control; things just occur anyhow. But the sovereignty of God means God rules over His creatures–He controls everything. **Things happen the way He wants or allows them.** *But our God is in the heavens: he hath done whatever he hath pleased* (Ps. 115:3).

God does not force His will on anyone and plots no evil, but He uses both good and evil occurrences to achieve His purpose.

For thou art not a God that hath pleasure in wickedness: neither shall evil dwell with thee (Ps. 5:4). *Let no man say when he is tempted, I am tempted of God: for God cannot be tempted with evil, neither tempteth he any man: But every man is tempted, when he is drawn away of his own lust, and enticed* (James 1:13-14).

If we truly believe in the sovereignty of God, we must see His hand in everything that happens to us. When people favor us, we see God working through them and when people mistreat us, we equally see God at work to bring blessings and glory out of the mischief. God prevails over the wicked and will turn their evil for your good, so do not let bitterness settle in your heart.

The wicked plots against the just, And gnashes at him with his teeth. The Lord laughs at him, For He sees that his day is coming. Their sword shall enter into their own heart, And their bows shall be broken. But You, O LORD, shall laugh at them; You shall have all the nations in derision (Ps. 37:12-13, 15; 59:8).

Your refusal to forgive denies your forgiveness from God and the joy of salvation–it imprisons you, makes you foolish and unfriendly, brings you into dishonor, shatters your dreams, and steals your peace and other blessings of God (Matt. 6:14-15; 18:34-35; Mark 11:25-26; Eccl. 7:9; Prov. 14:17a; 22:24; 25:23; cf. 16:32).

The prisoners of unforgiveness suffocate themselves with anger and create a toxic environment wherever they go. Consider the emotional tortures accompanying unforgiveness and determine not to give it a chance in your heart. Forgiveness is for your health, cherish it.

Chapter Three

AVOID FOOLISHNESS

The thought of foolishness is sin... (Prov. 24:9).

Foolishness is an inherent sin (*like pride*), and it cuts across all cultures and classes. *For from within, out of the heart of men, proceed evil thoughts... pride, **foolishness**...* (Mark 7:21-22). Most people will agree that pride is a serious barrier to cordial relationships, but may fail to see that foolishness does not make relationships pleasant, either. A fool is myopic and engages in wicked acts with impunity. *To do evil is like sport to a fool...* (Prov. 10:23).

A mad desire for self-gratification made Samson play with sexual immorality and cause distress to his nation while being an entertainer to his enemies (Judg. 15:10-11; 16:1, 4, 21, 25). It is risky working with a fool; his foolishness will frustrate you. *Let a man meet a bear robbed of her cubs, rather than a fool in his folly. If a wise man contends with a foolish man, whether the fool rages or laughs, there is no peace* (Prov. 17:12; 29:9).

> **Foolish actions entertain enemies but sting friends.**

Self-pride anchors foolishness. A fool is arrogant, self-deluded, or skeptical (Prov. 12:15a; 14:3a; Ps. 14:1; 1 Tim. 6:3-4). Foolishness is as sinful as pride. Children of God must denounce it and decisively deal with it rather than tolerate it. We all lived foolishly before our salvation but must discontinue that lifestyle, now that we are in the family of God where wisdom is accessible through Christ (Titus 3:3; 1 Cor. 1:30). *And an highway shall be there ... and it shall be called The way of holiness; the unclean shall not pass over it; but it shall be for those: the wayfaring men, **though fools, shall not err therein*** (Is. 35:8).

> **Foolishness is a moral disease.**

Foolishness is the blindness of the soul; it is the insensitivity of the mind (Ps. 119:70a; cf. Luke 24:25). A fool hates the truth, rejects godly counsel, and gropes in the dark. He disregards the wisdom of God and relies on his feelings, which fail him repeatedly. He does not admit his weaknesses and mistakes and thus keeps going in the ways of failure. *As a dog returns to his own vomit, so a fool repeats his folly* (Prov. 26:11).

A fool overly seeks attention and delights in high regard and can forgo his obligations to get it. He may engage in other people's responsibilities just to connect with them or get applause. He prefers ignorance, accedes to the demands of a crafty person and delightfully serves him (Prov. 15:21a; 11:29b; 2Pet. 3:5a).

> *A sucker is a pillar of the haughty.*

Wisdom is too high for a fool (Prov. 24:7a). He is a busybody and lives in strife (Prov. 18:6; 20:3; cf. 1 Pet. 4:15). He is full of words and speaks recklessly; he destroys himself with his own mouth as he cares for nothing except expressing himself (Eccl. 10:14a, 12b; Prov. 15:2b, 14b; 18:2, 7; 29:11a). *He who guards his mouth preserves his life, But he who opens wide his lips shall have destruction* (Prov. 13:3).

A fool can be simple-hearted or hard-hearted depending on the level of his foolishness (Prov. 1:22; 14:15a, 18a). Whether simple or hard-hearted, he is subject to deceit as he is comfortable with sycophants and hates truth-bearers: he assumes flattery for admiration, mockery for appreciation, lies for truth, and eventually loses his life in opposition to truth (Prov. 15:10, 12; 22:3; cf. 2 Chr. 18:5-7, 34).

> *Simple and hard fools are birds of a feather.*

A fool squanders resources (Prov. 21:20b). He despises instruction and is grief and calamity to his father and mother (Prov. 15:5a; 17:25; 19:13a; cf. Judg. 14:3; 16:30a, 31). God, our heavenly Father, did not put us on this earth without care and guidance. He gave us His Spirit and Word and instructed us to be obedient in order not to grieve His Spirit (Eph. 4:30; Ex. 23:20-21).

How often do we despise the Holy Spirit and grieve Him due to foolishness! Folly makes us neglect our duties and play riddles with our enemies; play the harlot with idols, and toy with

> *Foolishness goes hand in hand with ignorance.*

our consecration (Judg. 13:24-25; 14:12-13, 17; 16:16-20). Sinful lifestyles destroy the works of the Holy Spirit in our lives and hinder His power.

For My people are foolish, They have not known Me. They are silly children, And they have no understanding. They are wise to do evil, But to do good they have no knowledge (Jer. 4:22; cf. Hos. 4:6).

We are not to fear our enemies (Num. 14:9)*,* and neither are we to take them for granted. *For if a man finds his enemy, will he let him get away safely* (1 Sam. 24:19)*?*

An enemy hates and seeks the downfall of his prey (Ex. 15:9). He may cover his hatred with deceit and speak fair words but they are pitfalls, do not believe them (Prov. 26:24-25). Can a fool resist sweet words? He can only if he defies the pleasure of the moment, but he hardly considers the future.

An enemy only needs a little persistence with flattery and emotional blackmail to catch a hard fool and ruin his life (Judg. 14:16-17; 16:10, 13, 15-19); he can get a simple fool with just a disdainful smile. It takes a heart that abhors sinful lusts to distinguish between the wounds of a friend and the kisses of an enemy (Prov. 27:6). Oh, may a fool learn! Samson wasted his anointing and died with his enemies because of foolishness; he let his corrupt human nature silence the voice of God in his conscience (Judg. 16:20, 30). If not for foolishness, no human being– let alone a Christian will disobey God!

Case study: Let us use what happened between David and King Saul to explain how dependence on God toughens us against deceitful words and enables us to secure our divine position.

Saul was the first king of Israel, but God anointed David as the next king while he was still on the throne (1 Sam. 16:1, 13). *Better is a poor and a wise child than an old and foolish king, who will no more be admonished* (Eccl. 4:13). The young man David became a national figure when he fought and killed Goliath, the Philistine giant, who held the armies of Israel to ransom for 40 days (1 Sam. 17:31-32, 50).

Afterward, King Saul absorbed him into his army and made him captain of war (1 Sam. 18:2, 5). David's war victories sparked *dethronement anxiety* in the king and he became jealous of David (1 Sam. 18:6-9). All his plans to murder David failed because David behaved prudently and God's presence accompanied him (1 Sam. 18:11, 14; cf. 27:4).

David could kill Saul on two occasions, but he spared his life - this is real forgiveness. This moral act of David made Saul happy to the point of tears and he showered both praises and blessings on David, as shown below:

*So it was, when David had finished speaking these words to Saul, that Saul says, "Is this your voice, **my son** David?" And Saul lifted up his voice and **wept**. Then he says to David: "You are **more righteous** than I; for you have rewarded me with **good**, whereas I have rewarded you with **evil**. And you have shown this day how you have dealt **well with me**; for when the LORD delivered me into your hand, you **did not kill me**. For if a man finds his enemy, will he let him get away safely? Therefore may **the LORD reward you with good** for what you have done to me this day. And now I know indeed that **you shall surely be king**, and that the **kingdom of Israel shall be established in your hand**. Therefore swear now to me by the LORD that you will **not cut off** my descendants after me, and that you will **not destroy** my name from my father's house." So David **swore to Saul**. And Saul went home, but David and his men went up to the stronghold* (1 Sam. 24:16-22).

From the words in bold, you discover that Saul's statements were full of positive emotions and good words. He called David, son, shed tears of joy, condemned his own actions and justified David; prayed for God's blessings on David; acknowledged him as the next king, asked for his mercy on his family, and secured his oath. Based on these words that were sealed with a covenant, one expects that Saul's antagonism against David would cease.

> *Beware of sweet words, they're often snares.*

But our observation proved that the expectation was far from the truth, as Saul continued to hunt David. After David saved his life the second time, he said *...I have sinned. **Return**, my son David. For I will harm you **no** *more, because my life was precious in your eyes this day. Indeed I have played the **fool** and erred exceedingly* (1 Sam. 26:21).

Saul's soft words did not delude David, and neither did David trust Saul to reciprocate his kindness. A fool lacking discernment would have accepted the flattery as a peace treaty and would complain each time the king reneged on his promises until he slays him. David knew Saul would assassinate him if he had the opportunity, so he did not fall for his guaranteed security or or prayers and pronouncements. He trusted God's justice, placed his safety into God's hands, and went his way. This time, he left for the land of the Philistines that Saul could not invade because of enmity between the two nations.

> **You disappoint devil when you disdain the praises of mortals.**

*And David answered and said, "Here is the king's spear. Let one of the young men come over and get it. May the **LORD repay every man for his righteousness and his faithfulness**; for the LORD delivered you into my hand today, but I would not stretch out my hand against the LORD's anointed. And indeed, as your life was valued much this day in my eyes, so let **my life be valued much in the eyes of the LORD**, and **let Him deliver me out of all tribulation**." Then Saul says to David, "May you be blessed, my son David! You shall both do great things and also still prevail." So **David went on his way**, and Saul returned to his place* (1 Sam. 26:22-25).

*And David says in his **heart**, "Now I shall perish someday by the hand of Saul. There is nothing better for me than that I should **speedily escape** to the land of the **Philistines**; and **Saul will despair of me**, to seek me anymore in any part of Israel. So I shall escape out of his hand."* (1 Sam. 27:1).

It is important you weigh your actions in the light of God's love and wisdom as forgiveness is not synonymous with foolishness (Eph. 5:2a, 8b, 15), so you can know when to walk away (*mentally or physically*) from the wicked (cf. John 8:59). But this should not be out of fear or doubt about the ability of God to protect you or confirm His promises.

David's success offended Saul. Success exposes you to envy or jealousy–the Jewish authorities charged Jesus out of envy (cf. Gen. 26:14; 1 Sam. 18:7-9; Matt. 27:18). Not everyone will be happy for your success; many will resent you instead. David resisted intimidation, rejected carnality, and walked in discernment before and after he came into fame (1 Sam. 17:28-30, 33, 36, 38-40, 49-50, 57). If David had acted foolishly and failed, Saul would not have been jealous of him (Prov. 26:6; Eccl. 10:15).

Your achievement stirs up fear and insecurity in envious or jealous people and they see you as a threat to their position, privilege, or whatever.

You must be a fool failing in your divine assignment for you to get their kudos; otherwise, it is war, a bitter war that might be unlike the open war King Saul had against David. The aim of jealousy, whether in a bitter war or an open war, is destruction. Nothing could pacify Saul except the death of David, for *jealousy is cruel as the grave: the coals thereof are coals of fire, which hath a most vehement flame* (Song 8:6b).

...jealousy is the rage of a man: therefore he will not spare in the day of vengeance (Prov. 6:34). *Wrath is cruel, and anger is outrageous; but **who can stand before envy*** (Prov. 27:4)?

Saul was pursuing David for physical murder. Your own Saul might be after your spiritual death, not necessarily your physical death. His packaged deal will abort the plan of God for you if you accept his offer. Any of his weapons – flattery, money, or influence – can easily explode and kill you. *A man who flatters his neighbor spreads a net for his feet* (Prov. 29:5).

God can use anybody to favor or promote you, including your enemy, but do not jump to the conclusion that everyone who offers you help is God's sent; confirm from the Holy Spirit before you accept any offer. Would Saul ever have crowned David?

God, who is holy and establishes His children only in righteousness (Is. 54:14), already anointed David to replace Saul. *In thy name shall they rejoice all the day: and in thy righteousness shall they be exalted* (Ps. 89:16). Nobody could have nullified that divine appointment except David himself. And he would have done so by turning away from God's righteousness. Equally, God *has given to us all things that pertain to life and godliness* (2 Pet. 1:3; cf. 1 Cor. 3:21-23). The key to inheriting the **balanced** prosperity God designed for us in Christ Jesus is to prioritize the matters of His kingdom and righteousness in our life. *But seek ye **first** <u>the kingdom of God, and his righteousness;</u> and **all these** things shall be **added** unto you* (Matt. 6:33; cf. Prov. 8:20-21; 1 Chr. 4:9-10).

The righteousness of God is the spiritual characteristic that makes Christian relationships and transactions different from the world system. It leaves all doors open for the manifestations of God's promises and makes the believer inaccessible to Satan (1 John 5:18). Matthew (6:31-33) clearly shows that eternal salvation is the main blessing of God while material blessings are bonuses. We must, therefore, not crave material blessings more than spiritual blessings. A bonus does not have more value than its precursor.

For instance, if you buy five cups of rice and the seller gives you a handful of rice to appreciate your patronage, the handful of rice is not bigger than the five cups of rice and the seller did not give it to you before the purchase, but after. God knows your earthly needs and has pledged to provide them when you do the first thing first: trust Him and do your part.

Riches and honour; yea, durable riches and righteousness are the possessions of the righteous, not the wicked (Prov. 8:18; cf. 2 Cor. 8:9). Many children of God daily make themselves available for slaughter at the altar of foolishness for the sake of money, power, fame, or whatever. *For the turning away of the simple shall slay them, and the prosperity of fools shall destroy them* (Prov. 1:32).

Material prosperity without spiritual prosperity is incompatible with God's prosperity design for His children: the prosperity of the soul is at the topmost (3 John 2; cf. Deut. 28:1, 14). To reverse God's priority and pursue material things instead of God, is explicitly a vote of no confidence in God. *The fool hath said in his heart, There is no God* (Ps. 14:1a).

When we *usurp* God, we become bossy and interpret the Scriptures to suit us and commercialize our gifts. As 'industrious' bosses, we seek godfathers for connections and promotions, bully our fellow brethren, and take them as our employees/slaves (Matt. 24:49; cf. 1 Pet. 5:3a) rather than fellow laborers (Col. 4:11; Phil. 4:3; 1 Thess. 3:2; Philem.1:1, 24). And as 'successful' bosses, we become gods for the brethren to fear and obey, even when our command is an obvious contradiction to the gospel of Christ who purchased them with His blood (1 Cor. 7:23). Human worship is an inexcusable mistake, so both the hard and simple fools are culprits.

Having unseated God in the ministry, we welcome and roll with deadly enemies who initially appear peaceful and generous. These 'wonderful' friends and supporters stealthily and successfully plant their evil seeds in the ministry while we go about testifying the success of the ministry based on indicators such as the number of attendees, cash flow, and buildings.

Being deluded by covetousness, we conclude that material prosperity is an indicator of our spiritual competence and God's endorsement. Greed blindfolds her captives and they hardly see they are on the verge of eternal damnation (Jude 11; Phil. 3:18-19; cf. 2 Kin. 5:21-22, 25-27). Stay safe as a faithful steward (1 Cor. 4:2); the claim of God's ownership puts us in perpetual trouble.

Who is blind, but my servant? or deaf, as my messenger that I sent? who is blind as he that is perfect, and blind as the LORD'S servant (Is. 42:19)? Spiritual blindness and deafness make us feel confidence in falsehood. For example, we promote affluence as if it is a ticket to heaven, whereas no financial position guarantees right standing with God (cf. Ps. 62:9; Eccl. 7:14-15).

Both the righteous and the wicked can be rich or poor. The righteous might be bankrupt as the case of a true prophet who died in debt (2 Kings 4:1; cf. Rev. 2:9a) or as prosperous as the apostle, Barnabas, who sold his property to support poor brethren (Acts 4:36-37; cf. 14:14). Again, the wicked can be wealthy like Cain the murderer who built a city (Gen. 4:8-12, 16-17).

However, the prosperity of the wicked is a curse in disguise because he is out of God's presence. *When the wicked spring as the grass, and when all the workers of iniquity do flourish; it is that they shall be destroyed for ever* (Ps. 92:7; cf. Prov. 21:6). Riches, though pleasant, have no spiritual relevance, just like poverty (cf. James 1:9-11). In fact, without understanding, riches or poverty can ruin one's faith. This truth is more obvious in the prayer for adequate supply and contentment recorded in Proverbs (30:7-9).

Two things have I required of thee; deny me them not before I die: Remove far from me vanity and lies: give me neither poverty nor riches; feed me with food convenient for me: Lest I be full, and deny thee, and say, Who is God? or lest I be poor, and steal, and take the name of my God in vain.

Neither riches nor poverty make anyone righteous and they secure no privileges for anyone before God (Job 34:19; Deut. 10:17). All that matters in one's life is God's presence (Luke 16:22-23, 25). A foolish Christian trivializes the comfort of his soul and is in danger of exchanging his soul for wealth. The devil lies in wait for such ones and tricks them with possessions, so they care little or nothing about their spiritual state.

Judas Iscariot must have regarded himself as the richest among the apostles and thought of them as stupid for not devising ways to help themselves financially (John 12:4- 6). But who was stupid at the end: him or the other apostles? If not for foolishness anchored by sin, how can someone mortgage his eternal soul for material comfort that lasts a few years or prefer men's praise to God's honor (Mark 8:36-37; John 5:44; cf. 12:42-43)?

It is foolish to set out for a spiritual journey in faith with the Holy Spirit and end up in carnal arrangements and implementations. There are so many victims of foolishness to this day who make noise about doing God's work when they are spiritually dead and dry, and, in reality, accomplishing Satan's mandate. Who has beguiled us to think God will accept works done in the flesh? Who has deceived us into thinking material prosperity is a mark of true spirituality and lack of it an evidence of faithlessness and prayerlessness? Who has fooled us into thinking the care of our stomach is more important than the care of our soul?

Who has misled us into thinking the comfort of our body is more important than the comfort of our spirit? Who has deluded us into thinking physical comfort is the primary purpose of our salvation? Who has bewitched us to think God cannot add riches to us if we live in complete loyalty to Him? How can we prefer wealth to God?

Who has tricked us into thinking we can substitute obedience to God with any other thing? Who has deceived us into thinking the commendation of men signifies the approval of God? Who has beguiled us to think the flesh will lead us to eternal victory? Who has fooled us into thinking we can turn the gospel of Christ to personal/family business and go scot-free (Phil. 3:18-19; 2 Peter 20-21)? Who?

Let us consider the words below and repent of every carnally minded and foolish service.

O foolish Galatians! Who has bewitched you that you should not obey the truth, before whose eyes Jesus Christ was clearly portrayed among you as crucified? This only I want to learn from you: Did you receive the Spirit by the works of the law, or by the hearing of faith? Are you so foolish? Having begun in the Spirit, are you now being made perfect by the flesh? Have you suffered so many things in vain --- if indeed it was in vain (Gal. 3:1-4)?

All actions, whether good or sinful, begin with thoughts. We resolve what to do in our hearts before we do them. *As a man thinks in his heart, so he is* (Prov. 23:7a). You are as good or as bad as your thoughts and responsible for whatever thought you permit because the control of your heart is in your hand (Prov. 4:23).

You cannot desire to live a holy life and harbor evil thoughts, it will not work *for where your treasure is, there will your heart be also* (Matt. 6:21). Arrest thoughts that despise the righteousness of Christ in your heart and you will not fall victim to foolishness. Foolishness is evil and the foolish cannot have fellowship with God. *The foolish shall not stand in thy sight: thou hatest all workers of iniquity* (Ps. 5:5).

Chapter Four

BOLDNESS

...the righteous are as bold as a lion (Prov. 28:1).

Boldness is the ability to confront a problem without fear. It is not wildness, rudeness, or arrogance. Boldness enables you to humbly and calmly focus on your goal and accept nothing less than its fulfillment. As a Christian, your life goal is heaven and until you enter it, you have accomplished nothing.

The first step to victory is to welcome a challenge without fear. Boldness sends signals that intimidation will not work. Intimidation thrives in the clime of fear just as deceit prospers in the atmosphere of ignorance. Boldness does not accept an atom of timidity, no matter the obstacle.

Observe from the following cases that boldness strives ahead and does not hide. Jesus **went forth** and introduced Himself to the Jews who came to arrest Him but did not know Him in person; that act shocked His accusers (John 18:4-8). Every attempt the council of elders in the Synagogue made to stop Peter and John from preaching Christ became an opportunity for the disciples to tell them the truth to their faces (Acts 4:13, 19-20).

When David was to fight Goliath, he **ran forward** to meet the giant because he was fearless of his stature (1 Sam. 17:40, 48). The three young Hebrew men: Shadrach, Meshach, and Abednego, clearly told Nebuchadnezzar they would not bow to his idol despite his death sentence (Dan. 3:16-18).

Righteousness exudes boldness. *The wicked flee when no man pursueth: but the righteous are bold as a lion. A lion ... is strongest among beasts, and turneth not away for any* (Prov. 28:1; 30:30).

A righteous person does not succumb to defeat. You may not prevent or stop people from doing what they intend to do, but you can confront them by doing what the Holy Spirit has commissioned you to do. No matter how daunting it may seem, God will strengthen you to do what He has commanded (1 Thess. 5:24). Therefore, do not retreat in the face of any challenging situation.

> **Boldness is relentless.**

You do not win a battle by dodging or accommodating it, or by complaining about it. The problem remains and deepens if you respond in any of those ways. The power to win is within you–the righteousness of Christ in you. *For God hath not given us the spirit of fear; but of power, and of love, and of a sound mind* (2 Tim. 1:7).

After the death of Moses, God assured Joshua of His abiding presence that guarantees victories and encouraged him with this instruction: *Be strong and of a good courage* (Josh. 1:6, 9). Moses used the same word to encourage Joshua at his commissioning into leadership (Deut. 31:7). Jesus comforted His disciples with similar words in His parting speech: *Let not your heart be troubled, neither let it be afraid* (John 14:27).

> **Determination resists all oppositions.**

Such encouragement implies that despite God's guaranteed presence and victories, enemies and frightening situations will certainly arise in opposition and His children need to be fearless to subdue the oppositions and realize the victory (Matt. 10:26, 28, 31). Encouragement from others can only be useful to us when we internalize them. Otherwise, it will be of no effect.

> **Action proves decision.**

The phrase, *'Be strong and of a good courage'* repetitively occurs three times in Joshua chapter one alone (vs. 6, 9, 18). Let us emphasize the 'good' that qualifies the courage. Someone can be strong and of **bad** instead of **good** courage.

People who discover or accomplish great things by whatever means outside the righteousness of Christ are indisputably strong, but of bad courage. To *be of a **good** courage* is to be strong in the grace of God that enables us to do our jobs in the righteousness of Christ and have good success (2 Tim. 2:1; Joshua 1:8). **Bad** courage gives in to corruption while pursuing a goal and the outcome is bad success. The success is bad

> **Good success has virtues and eternal glory.**

because it lacks God's glory and leads to hell if the possessor, even if a household name, is unrepentant of his wicked ways before his death. *For what will it profit a man if he gains the whole world, and loses his own soul* (Mark 8:36).

This calls for caution for us to always incorporate holiness in our bravery, for without holiness, *no man shall see the Lord* (Heb. 12:14). Joshua became a great and successful leader in Israel because he resolved to shoulder the responsibility of good governance among people who often give in to complaints because of unbelief (Joshua 23:14; 24:29, 31; Numb. 14:26-27; Heb. 3:19).

Let us maintain strong and good courage throughout our tenure on earth so we can speak with confidence at the end of our ministry like Joshua, that we have achieved God's purpose and not ours (Josh. 23:14). Do not just be strong in speech. Be even stronger in actions. Action distinguishes the brave from the coward. Cowards do not have the stamina to take action because of fear. Their timidity makes them inactive *in the defense and confirmation of the gospel* and qualifies them as the first recipients of hell (Phil. 1:7, 17; Rev. 21:8).

> **The coward talks while the brave acts.**

Settle it within yourself not to entertain fear, whether of men or spirits, circumstances, or uncertainties and you will be unstoppable as you daily go about God's business. Fear is a satanic tool to disable your spiritual sight so you walk in doubt and pave the way for defeat (Matt. 14:30). There is nothing and nobody to fear when you fear God. People will rather fear you, for none can withstand God's presence in your life (Esth. 9:2-3; cf. Job 41:10b; Matt. 28:20b).

> **Enemies fear you when you fear God.**

There shall no man be able to stand before you: for the LORD your God shall lay the fear of you and the dread of you upon all the land that ye shall tread upon... (Deut. 11:25; cf. Matt. 18:6). *All power belongs to God* (Ps. 62:11), *and there is no wisdom nor understanding nor counsel against the LORD* (Prov. 21:30).

Fear God only. Hear it directly from our Lord Jesus.

And I say unto you my friends, Be not afraid of them that kill the body, and after that have no more that they can do. But I will forewarn you whom ye shall fear: Fear him [God], which after he hath killed hath power to cast into hell; yea, I say unto you, Fear him (Luke 12:4-5).

Chapter Five

PRAISES

Whoever offers praise glorifies Me... (Ps. 50:23). Who is like unto thee, O LORD, among the gods? Who is like thee, glorious in holiness, fearful in praises, doing wonders (Ex. 15:11)?

To praise God is to glorify Him for whom He is, and to be thankful for what He has done, is doing, and is yet to do. It is to ascribe to Him honor, power, and majesty. Praise is born out of a heart appreciative of the goodness received from another.

The gift of Jesus by whom forgiveness of sin and redemption is available to everyone made plain the kindness of God to humanity (John 1:29; 8:34, 36). Our salvation and other blessings we receive from God are out of His mercy. Destruction naturally awaits us. Therefore, do not take your position as a child of God for granted. People with a mentality of entitlement find it difficult to appreciate a gift and rather easily find fault with both the giver and the gift–Adam had this mentality after his fall (Gen. 3:12) and his children are like him till today.

The early apostles considered it honorable to be beaten for the sake of Christ and were thankful to God (Acts 5:40-41). Paul and Silas prayed and sang hymns to God while in prison, despite their beatings and unjust arrest (Acts 16: 23, 25). It is prestigious when one suffers not for crime but for the righteousness of Christ (1 Pet. 2:19). Regardless of whatever we experience, we should be grateful to God for adopting us in Christ (2 Tim. 1:8, 11-12). Praising God is not subject to feelings, but obedience to faith (1 Thess. 5:18). Anything not done in faith is sin (Rom. 14:23).

Our praise to God both in times of victories and adversities proves we are not at all doubtful of His sovereignty (Ps. 62:11; cf. Ex. 15:1-21). It is insulting to praise God only when we feel good. In any situation, we choose not to praise God, we grumble against Him. An appreciative heart cannot condone murmuring. This vice springs from a heart of unbelief and depicts man as being more righteous than God. Irrespective of man's opinion, God is excellent in justice: righteous in all His ways and at all times, infinite in wisdom and power (Job 12:13, 16; 37:23; Is. 40:13-14). He does great and unsearchable things (Job 5:9), and owes man no explanation (Job 33:13; cf. Rom. 9:20). We may not understand Him but it suffices us to believe Him.

When we try to use our little brain to figure out what God is doing, we may come to the wrong conclusion that He is doing nothing or that if He is doing anything at all, He is too slow. And we feel like giving Him counsel or yelling at Him rather than praising Him. Can the creature give wisdom to the Creator? Can the creature say to the Creator that He does not know what He is doing? *Shall the clay say to him who forms it, 'What are you making?' Or shall your handiwork say, 'He has no hands'* (Is. 45:9b; cf. Jer. 18:3-6)?

Who will deliver you if you are bitter against God? The elders of Israel who made complaint a habit perished in the wilderness, even though God intended to take them to the Promised Land–the land of great riches (1 Cor. 10:10; Num. 14:22-23; 26:64-65). If you are a grumbler, repent and engage in praise so that it will lift the spirit of heaviness off you; ashes will give way for beauty, and joy will take the place of mourning (Is. 61:3).

> **Praise is the medicine for a heavy heart. Why not praise now?**

God inhabits the praises of His people (Ps. 22:3), and thus, His presence lightens your heart while you praise. Praise deepens your trust in God and enables you to witness the power of deliverance and not destruction (Ps. 22:4). Songs of praises generated the power of God that collapsed the wall of Jericho (Josh. 6:20). The nations that came to attack Judah fought and destroyed themselves while the people of Judah were praising God (2 Chr. 20:21-23).

Chapter Six

DISARMED BY LOVE

Love does no harm to a neighbor; therefore love is the fulfillment of the law
(Rom. 13:10).

L ove is the most powerful weapon in warfare. It quenches wars without the aid of human ammunition and brings the warring factions to peace and unity, bringing about both earthly and eternal blessings (cf. Ps. 133:1, 3b).

Strife of all types and magnitudes results from hate. *Hatred stirs up strife, But **love** covers **all** sins* (Prov. 10:12). There is no hate in God. Love is His nature, just as hate is the nature of Satan. It is sad to say that none of us naturally has love. God's kind of love is true love. Adam had it, but lost it after his fall. Lust and hate occupied him thereafter and that corrupt nature is inherent in us from conception. *Behold I was shapen in iniquity; and in sin did my mother conceive me* (Ps. 51:5).

At a cursory observation, lust can be mistaken for love or its antecedent, and hatred seen as the outright opposite of love. But at a deeper consideration, lust only mimics love and is driven by selfishness. Love is always selfless; it grows and never gives up. Lust can initially push one to make tremendous sacrifices, but the tempo is only for a short period, whether its desire is met or not. In effect, both lust and hate stand in opposition to love.

> **Love grows, lust wanes.**

None of us can love ourselves, let alone love others, without the love of God operating in our lives. We may argue that no one hates himself, but anyone who does evil hates himself. Your hate for yourself shows in your hatred for others. If you truly love yourself, you will neither indulge in nor support sinful acts and will do no wrong to others intentionally. The Bible does not say, *love your neighbor **as he loves you.*** Instead, you are to *love your neighbor **as you love yourself*** (Matt. 22:39).

How can I love others when I engage in self-harming behaviors, treating myself with irreverence? Our fallen human nature is incapable of true love. Sin blinds us to this truth and we accuse one another as we search in vain for love. If love is a missing factor in our lives, that means we are without God, *for God is love* (1 John 4:8).

Our society is in a state of increasing chaos because it is godless; only the love of God can fix it. God already gave His love to the fallen and chaotic world through Jesus, His Son; and the only way the world will know this love is through believers in Christ.

*A new commandment I give unto you, That ye **love one another**: as I have loved you, that ye also love one another. By this shall **all men know** that ye are my disciples, if ye have love one to another (John 13:34-35). But I say unto you, **Love your enemies**, bless them that **curse** you, do good to them that **hate** you, and pray for them which **despitefully use** you, and **persecute** you; that ye may be the children of your Father which is in heaven: for he maketh his sun to rise on the evil and on the good, and sendeth rain on the just and on the unjust (Matt. 5:44-45).*

Love is a must, not an option for the followers of Jesus Christ in every generation. Only the love of Christ distinguishes a believer in Christ from the religious. Sinners live in hate and fight one another. *For we ourselves also were sometimes ... hateful, and hating others* (Titus 3:3). At the slightest offense, we say, 'You are looking for my trouble'. We voice it if the offender is of equal or lower status but may restrain from speaking when the offender is in a higher position. Whether spoken or not, the words denote that the offended has loads of trouble to dish out.

Love is the hallmark of Christianity, for by it God disarmed and defeated *Satan*, His and our enemy. As sinners, we had hatred and repaid evil to our offenders, but now, as Christians, we have love and are to offer it to our offenders in mercy. The Holy Spirit who lives in our spirit is the Spirit of God, whose is nature is love. He poured the love of God into our hearts to enable us to live in love and grow in love. *God's love has been poured into our hearts through the Holy Spirit who has been given to us* (Rom. 5:5).

We can only give what we have. Since we are now in possession of love, it is up to us to share it and be at peace with everyone, including our offenders (Rom. 12:18). We can say to our offenders, 'You are looking for my love' rather than 'You are looking for my trouble', for we no longer have trouble but love. We do not merely say it, but do it by overlooking the offense. We celebrate love every day when we relate to both our offenders and non-offenders without resentment. We will always pass the test of love with the mindset of sharing it wherever we go.

> **Christians are to celebrate love every day.**

Love is determined by action, not mere words (1 John 3:18). The core of love is to hold nothing against those who harm you or delight in your harm. Relating to people in love does not stop them from hating or hurting you. In fact, many will hate you without cause, but you must love them (Ps. 69:4; 35:12-14). *Owe no one anything except to love one another, for he who loves another has fulfilled the law* (Rom. 13:8). It is natural to love those who are kind to you, but true love is unconditional. You show it when you love those who despise and mistreat you (Luke 6:28, 32). God's love that flows **into** and **through** your heart (Rom. 5:5), helps you wrap up your behavior towards them.

> **You love as you keep forgiving.**

It is important to note that the love of God in your heart primarily transforms you and not the other person. Although your love may convict your offenders, they are at liberty to change. If someone, for instance, is a slanderer and speaks ill of you and you decide to forgive him and be kind to him, your forgiveness and kindness cannot make the person stop defaming you if he does not want to. You are the one who changed from being unforgiving to forgiving, and from unkindness to kindness.

Jesus knew from the beginning that Judas Iscariot was evil and would betray Him, but He allowed him the freedom to repent or be responsible for his own destruction (John 6:64, 70-71; 12:4-8; Matt. 26:21, 25; 27:3-5). Love changes you, but does not make you domineering. By attempting to control other people's behaviors, we put ourselves in a position that could lead to depression. The job of changing people's character is outside the scope of work God gave us. It is, therefore, impossible for us to accomplish it. God asked us to love people; it did not tell to transform people.

If you read the account of King Saul and David in the book of First Samuel (Chapters 18, 19, 20, 24, and 26), you discover that Saul never repented of his jealousy towards David despite all the values David added to his leadership and life. Change is divine and can be positive or negative. Anyone who turns from evil to good gets the grace of God, and whoever turns from good to evil gets the support of the devil. Why then should I love the offender if he is unwilling to change? You may ask.

A true understanding of love will release us from the feeling of entitlement in any relationship, including our nuclear family. The attitude of entitlement is simply pride. It makes us think someone must respond to us in a certain way because of what we do for them or who we are to them. And if it does not happen that way, we get offended and may decide to withhold our affection and services to them.

Is it not justifiable to expect every human being to reciprocate the love of God that He portrayed in Jesus for humanity to the point of shameful and painful death? Most often, people despise and insult God and yet, He loves them.

> *Loving, and not nagging service touches the heart.*

You will live in pure bliss and ignore ingratitude when you do away with an attitude of entitlement. Otherwise, your act of goodness declines and you become nonchalant even in your family duties. Love will not let you neglect your duties, despite the other person's discouraging responses. Love and pride cannot co-exist; one has to give way to the other. Here, you, a Christian, have to surrender pride for the love of God, which is in your heart to flow out. Love lays a platform for genuine relationships where we see people with the eyes of God, and feel for them with the heart of God.

Love is not blind; she sees clearly, but shows compassion rather than condemnation. God knows and sees all our sins and still allowed Jesus to die for us *while we were yet sinners* (Rom. 5:8), leaving the decision of

> *Love sees but overlooks.*

repentance to us. Walking in love makes us accessible just as wearing a veil made Moses approachable (Ex. 34:29-35). Every true Christian must wear the lens of God's love to serve people in the humility of Christ and in the power of the Holy Spirit.

Now, let us unveil love and closely look at her characteristics, using First Corinthians (13:4-7) as our leading Scripture [please read it for better understanding].

Love is long-suffering and kind. She is not envious. She does not boast or puff up about her good deeds but humbly recognizes the grace of God that made it possible (1 Cor. 15:10). She does not make God a liar by doubting His promises [*God be true, but every man a liar* (Rom. 3:4)]. She walks orderly and submits to authority. She is self-giving and does not hide necessary information from her dear ones (2 Cor. 6:11; John 15:15).

She is not ashamed of the object of her love (Gen. 2:25; Heb. 2:11). She is tolerant and forgiving and has no evil intentions; she forgives even without the offender's apology and leaves vengeance to God (Deut. 32:35). She blesses when cursed (Rom. 12:14): she relates to others the way she is and not the way they are.

Love gives people the benefit of the doubt. She does not discriminate; she loves everyone regardless of their pedigrees and character (Rom. 13:8; Luke 6:27). She neither does evil nor rejoices in evil. She harms no one, and neither does she delight in the plights of others. She keeps no record of evil and rewards evil with good (Rom. 12:21). She would rather be cheated than cheat others. She is not resentful, but peaceful.

> *Love doesn't overdo or underdo anything: she does things adequately.*

She does not complain, but prays. She gives freely. She counsels but does not control. She compliments but does not flatter. She competes with nobody. Her focus is on glorifying God (John 17:4). She never runs dry, grows old, or fails, for God is her Fountain. Her joy is in the salvation and well-being of others. She counts no costs in accomplishing Christ's great commission of soul-winning.

Actually, Christianity is all about the business of love. Jesus Christ came to market this love of God to humanity (Luke 2:49). He proved it with His death for the sins of man. Afterward, He handed the business over to His disciples (John 20:21; 17:20). Every Christian is, thus, a marketer of love.

> *Christianity is love business.*

As a marketer, you need to advertise your product in a way that attracts customers. Advertisers or marketers display their products at every available opportunity. Their commitment to promotions or sales is so high that they are unhampered by the indifference and discouraging attitudes of some prospective buyers. Their incessant persuasion increases both the awareness and acceptability of the products. People who previously might be uninterested in the product may eventually become customers and advertisers. As a result, the product gains popularity and higher demand.

On the strength of the above, as a marketer of love, your offenders or persecutors are your prospective customers. Target them and be determined to sell your product. Unless you lavish them with love, you may not get them. It cost God the blood of His only begotten Son, Jesus, to bring man back to Himself (Heb. 9:11-12). Jesus Christ endured great suffering and shameful death in the hands of the sinners He came to save (Heb. 12:2-3). The apostles suffered humiliation, imprisonment, and murder for the sake of the gospel of Christ (Acts 5:18, 40; 7:59; 9:23-25; 12:2, 4).

Unless we deny ourselves, we will find it absolutely difficult to follow the standard of the gospel business - love - set by God, the Owner of the business. Love is the difference between a Christian and those playing religion. Oppression truly hurts, but someone who relies on self for revenge is no different before God than the oppressor.

Even when the offended has justified reasons for fighting back, Love says, 'My child, forgive and don't revenge; I will handle it. You will hurt yourself the more if you choose to retaliate'. The Christian says, 'Yes Father' and relaxes, but the religious despises the instruction and goes on a rampage, driving himself farther away from the help of God. Anyone who heeds the voice of Love enjoys protection and gathers booties. Vengeance and recompense belong to God (Deut. 32:35). *If thy enemy be hungry, give him bread to eat; and if he be thirsty, give him water to drink: For thou shalt heap coals of fire upon his head, and the LORD shall reward thee* (Prov. 25:21-22; cf. 2 Kings 6:8, 21-23).

When we walk in love, our heart relaxes in God and is unworried of the wicked. The weapon of love makes the adversary either repent if they come to their senses (2 Tim. 2:25) or flee from us if they remain adamant (Prov. 28:1). The fear of the wicked shows we are not yet grounded in love. *There is **no fear in love**; but perfect love casts out fear, because fear involves torment. But he **who fears has not been made perfect in love*** (1 John 4:18).

> **Love dispels fear.**

Love is stronger than any weapon man has ever seen or is yet to see. It is the greatest weapon in warfare and the base of every spiritual labor: operating in spiritual gifts without love profits us nothing (1 Cor. 13:1-3; cf. Eph. 4:15). Love shows mercy and produces an effect when mercy goes with the truth. The interaction of mercy and truth activates the presence and power of God that changes all things for good.

> **Truth adds value when spoken in love.**

Mercy and truth are met together; righteousness and peace have kissed each other. Truth shall spring out of the earth; and righteousness shall look down from heaven. Yea, the LORD shall give that which is good; and our land shall yield her increase (Ps.85:10-12).

Love is eternal and the only quality that gives us access to the kingdom of God at the end of our service here on earth. Faith will give way to sight and hope to fulfillment but love remains forever for God is love (1 Cor. 13:8, 13; 1 John 4:8). The sole purpose of salvation is that we live with Christ now and forever (John 12:26; 1 Thess. 5:10;). Nothing could have made this union possible, except love, which the Holy Spirit poured into each of us at regeneration.

> **Love is the bedrock of life.**

We must examine our actions time after time to ensure they are based on love (1 Cor. 16:14). Actions speak louder than words. As a Christian, you ought to respond to your persecutors with love despite the magnitude of their offenses against you. We cannot fake love. Our character exposes us when we speak of love without demonstrating it in our transactions and relationships.

Prayer:

*Now God himself and our Father, and our Lord Jesus Christ ... make you to **increase and abound** in **love one toward another**, and **toward all men**, even as we do toward you: To the end, he may stablish your hearts unblameable in holiness before God, even our Father, at the coming of our Lord Jesus Christ with all his saints* (1 Thess. 3:11-13) in the name of Jesus. Amen.

Chapter Seven

WISDOM

How much better is it to get wisdom than gold... (Prov. 16:16).

Wisdom is the ability to handle a situation in a proper and rewarding manner. Wisdom is beyond education and falls outside the realms of humankind and animals (Job 28:12-14, 21). People cannot earn wisdom so no school teaches it (Job 28:15-18). It is a course available in the fear of God for everyone, whether at home, street, market, workplace, or city.

Wisdom cries out loudly to people at entrances for their benefits and eternal safety before they commit themselves to any activity (Prov. 1:20-23; cf. 8:1-4). Those who are attentive to her receive prudence and discretion to deal with day-to-day experiences. *...wisdom is profitable to direct* (Eccl. 10:10b).

Wisdom connect with knowledge and understanding. We can observe their unity in Proverbs (24:3-4; cf. 14:1) - *Through **wisdom** a house is built, And by **understanding** it is established; By **knowledge** the rooms are filled with all precious and pleasant riches.* Wisdom needs knowledge to build, but knowledge without understanding adds no value to wisdom.

Understanding is between knowledge and wisdom. It resides in the mind that abhors evil. Unless people comprehend what they see, hear, or say, they cannot correctly put it into practice–the correct usage of knowledge dependents on understanding. *Wisdom rests in the heart of him who has understanding. Understanding is a wellspring of life to him who has it.* (Prov. 14:33a; 16:22a).

Our behavior displays not only our wisdom but also its source. Wisdom is of two kinds: the wisdom of God, which is pure, peaceable, gentle, willing to surrender to righteousness, merciful, and diligent. And devilish wisdom characterized by bitterness, envy, strife, and sensuality; lies, hypocrisy, manipulation, intimidation, and control (James 3:14-17).

No one can purchase the wisdom of God. It is a gift of God obtainable in Christ–Christ is the wisdom of God (1 Cor. 1:24b; cf. Prov. 8). Whatever man considers wisdom outside Christ is nothing but foolishness garnished with deceit. *Professing themselves to be wise, they became fools* (Rom. 1:22).

God's wisdom is inexplicable, and we experience it only when we wholeheartedly represent and present Christ to the perishing world as the Son of God and the only Way to salvation. The antagonists of the gospel could not deny or withstand the wisdom in Stephen and Paul because Jesus Christ was their Attorney (Acts 6:9-10; 24:24-25). *Therefore settle it in your hearts not to meditate beforehand on what you will answer; for **I** [Jesus] will give you a mouth and **wisdom** which **all** your adversaries cannot **contradict or resist*** (Luke 21:14-15).

God's abiding presence follows you and makes you a dread to your opponents when you walk in His wisdom. The wisdom of God not only saved David from the cruelty of King Saul but also made David a terror to him.

*And Saul cast the spear, for he says, "I will **pin David** to the wall!" But **David escaped** his presence **twice**. Now **Saul was afraid of David**, because the **LORD was with him**, but had departed from Saul. Therefore Saul removed him from his presence, and made him his captain over a thousand... And David **behaved wisely** in all his ways, and the **LORD was with him**. Therefore when Saul saw that he behaved very wisely, **he was afraid of him*** (1 Sam. 18:11-15).

The wisdom of God, although more profitable with substance, elevates you above power and money. Power and money are husks to an individual with God's wisdom. *Wisdom is good with an inheritance: and by it there is profit to them that see the sun* (Eccl. 7:11). *Wisdom is better than **weapons of war**... Wisdom gives strength to the wise man more than **ten rulers** who are in a city. For the protection of wisdom is like the protection of **money**, and the advantage of knowledge is that **wisdom preserves the life** of him who has it* (Eccl. 9:18; 7:19, 12). *How much better to get **wisdom** than **gold**! And to get understanding is to be chosen rather than **silver**. Wisdom is the principal thing; therefore get wisdom: and with all thy getting get understanding* (Prov. 16:16; 4:7).

Excuses are hindrances to wisdom and easy routes to failures. God is not associated with failure, and it is unbecoming of us Christians to fail since we can freely receive wisdom from God if we faithfully ask Him. Failure involves improper behaviors such as laziness, time mismanagement, lack of vision, inadequate planning, and folly. God is never a part of them (Prov. 12:27; 6:6-11; 19:3).

> *Excuses bring forth failure or at best mediocrity.*

Our failure points to the fact we have not accepted our lack of wisdom or asked God for it in faith. *If any of you lacks wisdom, let him ask of God, who gives to all liberally and without reproach, and it will be given to him. But let him ask in faith, with no doubting, for he who doubts is like a wave of the sea driven and tossed by the wind. For let not that man suppose that he will receive anything from the Lord; he is a double-minded man, unstable in all his ways* (James 1:5-8).

Wisdom is a matter of the heart, not the head. Someone who relies solely on head knowledge might be great in talks but incompetent in generating solutions, and therefore serves *the wise of heart* whose words are usually few (Prov. 11:29; 17:27). **Anyone wrong in the heart cannot get it right in the head, and his hands will perform wrongly.** For us to get the right solutions, we first need a heart shift, then a mental shift resulting in an activity shift.

> *An upright heart generates right ideas.*

However, the wise that lacks reverence for God is altogether foolish because his wisdom stands on the wrong premise. Judas Iscariot must have regarded himself wise while he was pilfering from the group account and planning Jesus' betrayal, but soon realized he was a glorified fool, and then committed suicide (John 12:3-8; Matt. 26:21-22, 25; 27:35). *Do you see a man who is wise in his own eyes? There is more hope for a fool than for him* (Prov. 26:12).

*And to man He said, Behold, **the fear of the Lord**, that is wisdom, And to depart from evil is understanding* (Job 28:28). *The fear of the LORD is the beginning of wisdom: and the knowledge of the Holy One is understanding* (Prov. 9:10). *Where is*

> *The wise reverences God and departs from evil.*

the wise? where is the scribe? where is the disputer of this world? hath not God made foolish the wisdom of the world? For the wisdom of this world is foolishness with God. For it is written, He taketh the wise in their own craftiness (1 Cor. 1:20; 3:19).

The wisdom of God aligns with truth that does not contradict the Scripture, or the voice of God (John 17:17; Jer. 38:20). *Buy the truth, and do not sell it, Also wisdom and instruction* [knowledge] *and understanding* (Prov. 23:23). Unless we are determined to always measure our wisdom with the Scripture and heed the voice of the Holy Spirit, we will start walking in human wisdom, even while being zealous for the things of God.

Zeal without truth aborts missions and endangers lives. Josiah was one of the best and God-loving kings of Judah, but he died another man's death because he was not sensitive to the truth. In his eagerness to fight an enemy, he failed to discern the voice of God restraining him from the battle (2 Chr. 34:1-2, 31; 35:20-24).

God works in mysterious ways (Is. 55:8-9). We can only remain and progress in His wisdom if we constantly humble ourselves to learn even from ants (Prov. 6:6). Human wisdom, which is earthly and devilish, expands one's ego, misleads, and brings losses in the end, but God's wisdom keeps you growing in humility (cf. John 7:2-6, 10).

Our ability to detect the wisdom of God at all times and in all matters depends on how much we seek the truth and closely interact with God's Spirit. The Holy Spirit not only reveals to us the blueprint; He leads us step by step to accomplish it. He gives us specific instructions on what to do, when to do it, how to do it, where to do it, and with whom to do it if necessary (Ex. 31:1-6; Acts 16:6-10). He regulates our wisdom with truth and we can avoid blunders as long as we heed His voice.

Although *wisdom is profitable to direct* (Eccl. 10:10b), we are not to pride ourselves on wisdom but in the all-wise God who gives us the right knowledge, understanding, and application. *Thus saith the LORD, Let not the wise man glory in his wisdom ... but let ... him glory in this, that he understandeth and knoweth me, that I am the LORD which exercise lovingkindness, judgment, and righteousness, in the earth: for in these things I delight, saith the LORD* (Jer. 9:23-24).

Chapter Eight

NO IDOLS

Little children, keep yourselves from idols (1 John 5:21).

An idol is anyone or anything we put first in our lives and depend on, rather than God. Human beings have the inclination to walk by sight instead of faith. They are more likely to believe what they see, feel, hear, smell, or touch as compared to what they cannot. As a result, they deify man and other living or non-living things rather than worship God (Acts 14:11-15; 8:8-11; Dan. 5:4; Rev. 9:20); put their trust in the leaders, or preachers of the gospel rather than in God who installs the leaders/sends the preachers (1 Cor. 3:4-7); stick to familiar but futile method instead of seeking God for new and genuine approach (Heb. 7:18-19).

Even when they declare allegiance to God, their obedience sometimes is not from a perfect heart. That is why they quickly turn away from God in the absence of His faithful representatives. For instance, the people of Israel worshipped God in the presence of Moses but bowed down to a calf in his absence (Ex. 32:1-6). King *Joash* (of Judah) *did that which was right in the sight of the LORD all the days of Jehoiada the priest*, but after the death of Jehoiada, he left *the LORD God and served groves and idols* (2 Chr. 24:2, 17-18). The disciples of Christ went back to their former occupation, fishery, after Jesus' ascension (John 21:2-3), although they repented wholeheartedly afterward.

Do you walk by sight or by faith? Where do you set your heart? Who does your mind first go to when you are seeking a solution—God, a person, or knowledge? Give honest answers to these questions to ensure you have no other god before God (Ex. 20:2-3).

God is omniscient and *a very present help in trouble* (Ps. 46:1). We restrict the all-knowing God from helping us when we trust in man, knowledge, or skills to solve a problem. There is nothing too little for the devil to oppose, and we cannot overcome him without leaning on God. We decode his secrets and foil his plans only when we rely on God.

We despise the mercy of God and abuse His grace when we depend on other sources. David, the second king of Israel, was a man very dependent on God. He always sought God's face for ways of approaching new problems and, because of this, won all his wars and accomplished many things. Although he got the desired results from God's previous instructions, he never relied on such experiences when faced with fresh problems. We are most likely to fail if we go our way to execute a project with the notion that God will grant us victory simply because He did it before.

...The LORD is with you while you are with Him. If you seek Him, you will find him; but if you forsake Him, He will forsake you (2 Chr. 15:2). God does not impose Himself on us; He handles only what we commit to Him. *Commit your way to the LORD, Trust also in Him, And He shall bring it to pass* (Ps. 37:5).

On one occasion, the Amalekites invaded Ziklag and carried away both David's and his armies' wives and children while they were away at war. When they came back, David did not immediately embark on a war against the Amalekites with the presumption of victory. He did not employ logic.

For instance, it is logical to think that God would grant David victory over Amalek who attacked his immediate family and community since He gave him victory over the Philistines when he warred against them in defense of the people of Keilah, a distant relative (1 Sam. 23:1-5). But David did not fight the Amalekites until he inquired from God what to do (1 Sam. 30:8). He went to war against them with great strength and confidence as God said to him: *...Pursue, for you shall surely overtake them and **without fail** recover all.*

We engage in trial and error when we depend on knowledge or skill. No matter how brilliant we are, we can never be accurate without God. We can get mind-blowing results from our activities, but not miracles from God when Mr. Ambitious Flesh stirred the undertakings! The Spirit of God altered the plan of Paul and his team to preach in Asia and Bithynia and directed them to Macedonia where they cast out the spirit of divination from an enslaved girl, resulting in their battering and imprisonment. However, God confirmed their works with great miracles as His power collapsed the prison security and gathered souls for salvation (Acts 16:6-10, 16-18, 22-23, 25-34).

Paul discontinued his arrangement and followed God's instruction. He would not have perceived God's disapproval had he glued to experiences. Paul's attitude should challenge us to the intimacy of fellowship with the Holy Spirit so that we can always discern His voice and cancel any plan that lacks the approval of God, however good it appears. We run our own course and convert the Gospel to personal trade when we rely solely on experiences. This is one of the main reasons many missionary works have little or no impact.

Regardless of the magnitude of our achievements, we should not rely on our ability, experience, or any other thing if we must not fall into the trap of idol worship. God does not contest for the number one position in our life, it is rightfully His. Anything or anyone that occupies that position becomes our god whom we worship and trust to our own hurt and shame (Jer. 25:7, Is. 30:3).

> **God is willing to give you fresh experiences; let Him.**

Woe to those who go down to Egypt for help, And rely on horses, Who trust in chariots because they are many, And in horsemen because they are very strong, But who do not look to the Holy One of Israel, Nor seek the LORD! Now the Egyptians are men, and not God, And their horses are flesh, and not spirit. When the LORD stretches out His hand, Both he who helps will fall, And he who is helped will fall down; They will perish together (Is. 31:1, 3).

Chapter Nine

SELF-DEFENSELESS

The LORD of hosts shall defend them… (Zech. 9:15).

Regardless of what people do to a dead man, he can never rise to defend himself. Whether they slap, knock, or beat him, he lies there helpless, however strong he was when alive. People who could not stand his gaze while alive can do to him whatever they want without getting a reaction from him.

Similarly, you are a dead person in Christ; your very person died with Christ the day you accepted His death for your sins and received His own life. *Know ye not, that so many of us as were baptized into Jesus Christ were baptized into his death* (Rom. 6:3)?

Your conscious refusal to vindicate yourself is what proves your death to living for yourself. The difference between you and the physically dead is your free choice; the dead man does not have options to pick from.

You do not conceive all your righteous actions that offend people but by the Holy Spirit. You are only an instrument. Explain when necessary, but you might not convince your audience (Acts 22:22- 23). Unless the Holy Spirit who acts through you reveals the matter to them, they cannot understand and will not believe you.

What amount of explanation do you think Mary would have given her fiancé, Joseph, for him to believe her pregnancy was by the power of the Holy Spirit (Luke 1:35)? How do you think Joseph, an enslaved boy, would have explained to his master, Potiphar, that he was innocent of his wife's rape accusation (Gen. 39:19)? What explanation do you think Elijah would have given to the Israelites for them to believe he had the support of God for the three and half years of drought he pronounced against the land (1 King 17:1; James 5:17)?

Given these examples, relax in God's care and love when you do His will, for He shall appear on your behalf at His appointed time (1 Pet. 5:6-7). He knows 'when' and 'how' to defend you. Job's several answers to the accusations of his three friends for his predicament did not change their attitude towards him; rather, they mocked him even more. To them, such indescribable sufferings could not be the lot of the righteous (Job 21:1, 3; 4:7). God did not defend Job until He deemed it fit. When He judged Job and his friends, He declared the friends guilty, acquitted Job, and made him priest over them (Job 42:7-9).

God is in charge both in heaven and on the earth; the hearts of all people are in His hands and He deals with them according to His pleasure (Ps. 135:6; Prov. 21:1; 19:21). As He proved Mary innocent when her fiancé was contemplating to call off the engagement, so will He defend you (Matt 1:19, 20).

He, who vindicated Joseph will vindicate you (Gen. 41:14, 38). He, who showed His support for Elijah's actions by answering with fire when he called upon Him will defend your actions (1 Kings 18:36, 38). He that caused Haman to be hanged in the gallows he made for Mordecai will turn your situation around (Esther 7:9-10).

Your defense is of God who saves the righteous (Ps. 7:10); therefore, **do not be afraid.**

Chapter Ten

PATIENCE

By your patience possess your souls (Luke 21:19).

We commence our journey with Christ by faith, but lay hold of our possessions in Him by patience. You lose your soul to possessions if you bypass patience to get them. *...do not become sluggish, but imitate those who through faith and **patience** inherit the promises* (Heb. 6:12).

Patience is the ability to persevere in the face of adversity or unfortunate conditions with calm and contentment. It is the ability to endure pains, hardships, trials, and delays cheerfully. Patience **actively waits** for the Lord; she delightfully does the things within her reach while trusting God for those beyond her. Patience is **not passive acceptance of fate**. It is not being gloomy and recoiling in utter disappointment. It does not involve negligence of one's duties or doing them inattentively or in anger.

> *Patience is productive while waiting.*

When you have done everything to the best of your ability and a particular situation remains unchanged, let patience have its way. *For you have need of endurance, so that after you have done the will of God, you may receive the promise* (Heb. 10:36). Accept your limitations as a human being; you cannot save yourself from any situation. Do what you can; what you cannot do, God can and will - if you allow Him. Attaining an impossible thing is only possible with God (Mark 10:27).

God may seem late, but He is never late to intervene in any situation (Hab. 2:3). He does not rush into events as He contends with no one. He sometimes allows the oppressors to exhaust their plans: to come to a point where they feel that nobody can deliver the oppressed from their hands or the situation (2 Chr. 32:14; Dan. 3:15; cf. Is. 49:24-25).

> *Do what you can and leave what you can't to God.*

For instance, God did not rescue Peter the apostle from the hand of Herod until the night before his execution (Acts 12:6-11). Shadrach, Meshach, and Abednego experienced God's deliverance right inside the inferno (Dan. 3:23, 25). Daniel witnessed God's deliverance in the lion's den (Dan. 6:22). God moved Ebed-Melech to speak on his behalf Jeremiah only when Jeremiah was in a dungeon filled with mire (Jer. 38:6-7, 12-13). The sealed tomb and the guards could not prevent the resurrection of Jesus Christ on the third day–the set day of God before the foundation of the world (Matt. 27:66; 28:2, 4; Acts 2:23-24).

Considering these cases, it is better to wait patiently whenever an answer to your request seems delayed. The ever-present God (Ps. 46:1) does not need our timing to intervene because He acts only in His time, which nothing or no one can alter. He is not silent to those who wait in faith for Him (Ps. 40:1). During the waiting period, He perfects things preceding the miracle which we are usually unaware of. Therefore, shun impatience and do nothing out of desperation.

Be anxious for nothing.

Human efforts fail. Until God's set time for your deliverance comes, all your efforts to liberate yourself appear ineffective (Ps. 105:19*).* Joseph tried in vain to secure human help to get out of prison. Having interpreted a favorable dream to Pharaoh's chief butler, he requested him to mention his case to Pharaoh, but two years elapsed before the butler could remember him (Gen. 40:14; 41:1, 9). The chief butler forgot Joseph because God was still working out things that would culminate in the miracle He had for Joseph. The greatest thing the chief butler, in his capacity, may have done for Joseph was to secure his release from the prison. Being a slave and a foreigner, securing his freedom will lead him to destitution. Of what glory would it have been to God if Joseph, after his release, loitered on the streets of Egypt?

Desire earnestly, the infinite help of God. Man's help is limited. Man lacks the power for definite solutions. *Put not your trust in princes, nor in the son of man, in whom there is no help* (Ps. 146:3). His help brings you out of one problem only to land you in another that often is more complex than the former. King David understood this and prayed: *Give us help from trouble, For the help of man is useless. Through God we* *will do valiantly, For it is He who shall tread down our enemies* (Ps. 60:11-12).

Wait patiently for God and receive your perfect deliverance with great honor. Hear what the Scripture says: *For since the beginning of the world Men have not heard nor perceived by the ear, Nor has the eye seen any God besides You, Who **acts** for the one who waits for Him* (Is. 64:4). *Whoever keeps the fig tree will eat its fruit; So he who waits on his master will be honored* (Prov. 27:18). *...If anyone serves Me, him My Father will honor* (John 12:26).

Like Job, determine to wait until your change comes (Job 14:14). The honor will be far above your expectations and the imaginations of others. Joseph was only concerned about being released from prison (Gen. 40:14), probably to get a menial job afterward. But God, who had been watching his ordeal from his father's house, had a grand plan for him. When it was the set time to confirm the accuracy of his dreams, God caused Pharaoh to have dreams (Gen. 37:6-7, 9; 41:1, 14).

God's purpose for Joseph was leadership, but he needed experience to acquaint himself with the skills necessary for righteous governance. While passing him through the training, God was also directing his footsteps to the place of his primary assignment. In the prison, he received the last batch of the leadership drill. On finding him faithful to the end, God lifted him from prison to the position of Prime Minister in Egypt: a land of his captivity. Joseph had all the authority to run the government; Pharaoh was only the ceremonial head (Gen. 41:38-44).

Persevere until it is over; no barrier can stand against what God destined for you. The Almighty God who will perform it had declared: *...who would set the briers and thorns against me in battle? I would go through them, I would burn them together* (Is. 27:4). God will deliver you from that difficulty as you keep on trusting Him. You may ask, 'When, and probably, how?' My answer is, 'I don't know'. But one thing I know is that *God is not a man, that He should lie, Nor a son of man, that He should repent. Has He said, and will He not do? Or has He spoken, and will He not make it good* (Num. 23:19)? His mouth has spoken it and His hand alone will perform it (2 Chr. 6:4).

Consider the case of Joseph and several others in the Bible. He who exalted Joseph to the position of power in a foreign land where he entered not as a freeman but as a slave will exalt you. Believers are foreigners in this world. We are

here because God wants to use us to bring many more sinners into His kingdom. Allow Him to train you for the office He has called you into, so you will be productive and make a difference in your generation and beyond. No one who trusts and hopes in God suffers disappointment at the end (Is. 40:30-31).

All the good things of life are the portion of people who revere and seek God (Ps. 34:9-10). However, impatience deprives them of God's perfect solution and desperation makes them enslave themselves to get what is rightfully theirs. Anything done in desperation always results in a catastrophe and poses a threat to your eternal salvation. As a good soldier of Christ, you must endure hardship and be content with what you have (2 Tim. 2:3; Heb. 13:5; cf. 1 Tim. 6:6) *so* you will not cheapen your Christian life for

any reason. Jesus bought you with His priceless blood, your worth is beyond every currency and anything the world can offer.

As much as patience is active and not passive, we must be careful what we do in the waiting period. We can claim to be waiting for God when, in reality, He is waiting for us. Sometimes we indict God for delayed intervention when we are the ones delaying His intervention. Let us consider three cases to prove our point.

1) <u>The birth of Isaac</u>

After Abraham had a wonderful communion with God in which God reassured him of His promise to give him a son, he accepted the misguided counsel of his wife, Sarah, and slept with Hagar, their maid. His union with Hagar produced Ishmael (Gen. 15; 16:3-4, 15). There was no intimacy between Abraham and God during this period, although his faith was still in God. After a while, God reminded him of His faithfulness and asked him to walk holily. *When Abram was ninety-*

nine years old, the LORD appeared to Abram and says to him, "I am Almighty God; walk before Me and be blameless" (Gen. 17:1). Ishmael was fourteen years old when Isaac was born (Gen. 16:16; cf. 21:5). Had Abraham not accepted Sarah's ungodly counsel, they might not have waited for twenty-five years before the birth of Isaac.

2)   Freedom from slavery

God told Abraham that his descendants were to stay in Egypt for 400 years before their deliverance, but they stayed 430 years (Gen. 15:13; cf. Ex. 12:40).

3)   Journey to the Promised Land

Israelites were to get to Canaan within 11 days after they had spied on the land, but it took them 40 years (Deut. 1:2; cf. Num. 14:33-34).

Who delayed who in all these cases? Imagine the pains we cause ourselves when we delay God because of compromise, ignorance, or disobedience (cf. Ps. 81:13-16)! **Carnal arrangements put God on hold**.

Chapter Eleven

BEING PRAYERFUL

For we wrestle not against flesh and blood, but against principalities, against powers, against the rulers of the darkness of this world, against spiritual wickedness in high places (Eph. 6:12).

As Christians, we already know we pray to God through Jesus. *If ye shall ask any thing in my name, I will do it* (John 14:14). *Then Peter said ... In the name of Jesus Christ of Nazareth rise up and walk. And he took him by the right hand, and lifted him up: and immediately his feet and ankle bones received strength. And he leaping up stood, and walked...* (Acts 3:6-8).

Our opening Scripture tells us to direct all our fights against evil spirits. We must have nothing against any human but all things against the devils if we are to be successful in prayer warfare. Satan and his demons are the principal agents of persecution who instigate ignorant foolish men (1 Pet. 2:15) to fight against the righteousness of God. They are evil spirit beings–persons without bodies; the masterminds of all evil happenings in the world. We prevail against them in prayer through the name of Jesus and not any other name or carnal method.

For though we walk in the flesh, we do not war after the flesh: (For the weapons of our warfare are not carnal, but mighty through God to the pulling down of strong holds;) Casting down imaginations, and every high thing that exalteth itself against the knowledge of God, and bringing into captivity every thought to the obedience of Christ (2 Cor. 10:3-5).

Prayer is a spiritual activity because the God to whom we pray is a Spirit, and the devils we pray against are spirits as well. We too have to be in the spirit to connect to God in the spiritual realm through the Holy Spirit (John 4:24; cf. Rom. 1:9). Our spirit is the inner sanctuary where the Holy Spirit dwells and we have to liaise with Him to be above evil spirits

(1 Cor. 3:16; 6:19; cf. Acts 17:24). We can pray anywhere, provided we are spiritually conscious.

There is no structured manner of praying (1 Sam. 1:10, 13; Ps. 63:6; Ezek. 9:8; Josh. 7:6; Matt. 26:39; John 11:38, 43; Acts 3:4, 6; 4:24). Pour out your heart to God in a way or language most suitable to you as inspired by the Holy Spirit (Ps. 62:8b). We really do not know what and how to pray, but the Spirit of God helps our inadequacy in prayer, and guides us according to God's will (Rom. 8:26-27). You speak your mind to God in prayer as a child would talk with his father when you do not pray in any conventional method. Prayer could be as requests, thanksgiving, praise, intercession, meditation, or warfare.

God has power over all His creation but He is just in His dealings and does not compromise His standard. For us to get His intervention in all the things that bedevil us in this life, we must live in the righteousness of Christ and exercise the Christian authority in prayer over everything that contradicts His eternal decrees (Matt. 10:7-8; Mark 16:17-18). *I will therefore that men pray every where, lifting up **holy** hands, **without wrath and doubt*** (1 Tim. 2:8).

Prayer goes hand in hand with the word of God, which is the **sword** of the Spirit (Eph. 6:17). The word of God is a two-edged sword used in prayer to defeat evil spirits, sicknesses, diseases, infirmities, death, and other problems (Ps. 149:6-9; 147:15). Praying according to the Scriptures (will of God) coupled with holiness results in answered prayer. ...*The effectual fervent prayer of a righteous man availeth much* (James 5:16).

The prayer of the ungodly is not only ineffective, it causes a backlash like with the seven sons of Sceva who the demons they were casting out wounded because they were living in sin and had no relationship with Jesus and thus, lacked His authority (Acts 19:13-16). The prayer of the sinful does no damage to the kingdom of darkness, as it lacks the power of God.

We put everything in the right perspective through prayer. No one can survive in any kingdom service without prayer that is in line with God's word and will; prayer is the breath and foundation of all ministries (Acts 6:4). The strength of a Christian depends on the degree to which he applies the authority of Christ in prayer.

We will lose the strength to accomplish anything eternally good if we do not humble ourselves before God through constant, sincere prayer. The instruction to *pray without ceasing* remains as valid to us today as it was when Paul gave it

> *The humble seeks the face of God, the proud don't.*

to Christians at Thessalonica (1 Thess. 5:17). People who acknowledge human frailty pray; the arrogant sees no need for prayer (Ps. 34:17; cf. Job 21:15).

Although we can pray at all times and anywhere, it is beneficial to map out specific times to be alone with God, especially late at night or early in the morning, when natural activities will not interrupt your conversation with Him (Ps. 42:8; Mark 1:35; Luke 5:16). Such times are the best times to reflect on your previous activities and commit your life and all your plans afresh to God.

We received the grace of God to do His will at regeneration but renew it daily in prayer and by obedience grow in it (Rom. 1:5; cf. John 1:16-17). Man is by nature accustomed to doing evil and unless a believer is constantly decisive in

> *A believer who prays and obeys grows in God's grace.*

prayer to say **'no'** to falsehood, ungodliness, and worldly lusts, his corrupt self-desires will obstruct the growth of grace in his heart (Heb. 13:9; Titus 2:11-12). Ceaseless submission to God in prayer wins the battle of living right in the world where the majority surrender themselves to wickedness and despise those who do good (2 Tim. 3:3).

We receive strength in prayer when we resolve to obey God. Our Lord Jesus prevailed over the devil at Gethsemane, not Golgotha. He prayed there until the exceeding sorrow in his soul vanished, and His weak body strengthened to do the will of God (Mark 14: 34, 38, 41-42). Then, He became bold enough to face the problems which before that time, were threats to Him.

> *Prayer and right action make things real.*

Gentle dispositions result from earnest prayer. If He had not firmly decided in prayer to surrender to the will of God, He would have resisted the crucifixion. We receive victory in prayer, but actualize it by action.

Prayer does not replace obedience. We should do whatever God tells us in prayer (Acts 13:1-3). If we conclude on what to do in a particular situation before seeking the face of God in prayer, He either ignores us or answers us according to our plans, which will certainly disappoint us (Ezek. 14:4, 7-8; Jer. 42:19-22). *If I regard iniquity in my heart, the Lord will not hear me* (Ps. 66:18).

Praying without obeying instructions from God is a sheer waste of time and energy. Soliciting prayers here and there without willingness and readiness to submit to God's counsel also profits nothing, as feelings do not move God but faith. The intention of prayer is not to present our proposals to God for approval or to seek attention from others, but to do His will. Prideful and hypocritical prayers are nothing but drama: Jesus condemns them (Luke 18:9-14; Matt. 6:5-7).

It is an error to think God will influence our actions when we have not genuinely and completely surrendered our will before Him in prayer. There is no limit to what we can ask God in prayer once it agrees with His will. We can, therefore, faithfully ask Him to help our unbelief, which makes us doubt His goodness (Mark 9:24). He will grant our request because it is His will that we believe Him.

*Ask, and it shall be given you; seek, and you shall find; knock, and it shall be opened unto you. And **all** things, **whatsoever** you shall ask **in prayer**, believing, you shall receive (Matt. 7:7; 21:22). Now this is the confidence that we have in Him, that if we **ask anything according to His will**, He hears us* (1 John 5:14).

Until you have peace concerning a particular matter, do not stop praying about it. Jesus continued in prayer till He had peace within Him: *And being in agony he prayed more earnestly...* (Luke 22:44). Let us not behave like the disciples who went to sleep because of sorrow, instead of praying to overcome whatever caused the sorrow. *And when he rose up from prayer, and was come to his disciples, he found them sleeping for sorrow* (Luke 22:45).

Whenever you feel sorrowful, whether for known or unknown reasons, pray till the sorrow disappears. Hannah, who could not eat because of the bitterness of her soul, became cheerful after prayer (1 Sam. 2:7-8, 10, 18). When the Lord found His disciples sleeping He said to them: *Why do you sleep? Rise and pray, lest you enter into temptation* (Luke 22:46).

As the Lord spoke to His first set of disciples, so He speaks to us - His disciples today! Let us, therefore, pray always that we may prosper in our Christian faith and remain triumphant as we share testimony after testimony.

Miracles are daily experiences of God's children, and problems make you a potential candidate for them. You realize miracles not by worry, fear, or grumbling, but by fellowship with God the Holy Spirit in genuine prayer of faith. Nothing is too little or big to pray about. God cares. *Be careful for nothing; but in every thing by prayer and supplication with thanksgiving let your requests be made known unto God* (Phil. 4:6).

It is important to note that prayer from an unforgiving heart does not get the attention of God (Mark 11:25-26). You cannot pray rightly without forgiveness. Some Christians pray for the death of their enemies and justify this witchcraft because their presumed enemies are demons and not humans. But this shows how deluded they are. Demons are spirits, and spirits cannot die. You can cast out evil spirits, destroy their works, and free their captives, but you cannot kill them (Mark 16:17; 1 John 3:8).

You work against yourself and promote your human enemies when you delight in their disasters. *Do not rejoice when your enemy falls, And do not let your heart be glad when he stumbles; Lest the LORD see it, and it displease Him, And He turn away His wrath from him* (Prov. 24:17-18).

Showing attitudes of care and concern toward your adversaries qualifies you to be a candidate whom God Himself will celebrate in their presence. Therefore, desire no evil against them if you want God to honor you (cf. Ps. 35:12-14). God knows how best to handle the wicked, leave them to Him (Job 40:11-14). *You prepare a table before me in the **presence of my enemies**; You anointed my head with oil; My cup runs over* (Ps. 23:5)!

What a great honor for God to exalt you before your enemies! God humiliates them with your exaltation and perhaps some of them repent. What glory to depopulate the kingdom of darkness through your tenacity in right prayers! God blessed Solomon much more because he did not ask for the death of his enemies but for wisdom and knowledge to do his work (2 Chr. 1:11-12).

You will be free from bitterness if you sincerely pray for people who hurt you. Jesus interceded for His persecutors, setting the standard for us (Luke 23:34). Stephen emulated our Lord Jesus as he asked God to overlook the sins of his murderers (Acts 7:60). You cannot genuinely intercede for others if you bear grudges and have no compassion for them. Our flesh still runs with natural life, and will always want to have its way. If we do not bring it under control in constant prayer, we will prefer our own ways and serve God according to the evil imaginations of our heart (Jer. 16:12). With such a deceived heart, we can endorse whatever God disapproves of and still claim to be obedient to God. When we resolve in prayer to do the will of God, vengeance becomes unfit for consideration, since God will vindicate and avenge us.

We lack inner strength for good works when we faint in prayer or pray outside the will of God. Hence, we engage in witchcraft or physical combat with people. Our inability to respond to our persecutors in the similar manner our Lord Jesus responded to His accusers is a proof we are not following His pattern of prayer - *who, when He was reviled, did not revile; when He suffered, He did not threaten, but **committed Himself** to Him who judges righteously* (1 Pet. 2:23).

God, who commands us to pray, has promised to answer us (Ps. 91:15). So follow His instructions while you pray in order to get your desires.

Chapter Twelve

NO APOLOGY

The evil bow before the good; and the wicked at the gates of the righteous
(Prov. 14:19).

In humility, accept your faults whenever you do wrong and apologize without waiting for the offended to demand it. But do not regret your actions when you do no evil and someone feels insulted because you obeyed God. Disobedience is not sinful when the holiness of God is intact. When you obey God, you offend not man but the devil (Acts 25:8*)*.

God created everyone to worship and obey Him (Is. 43:21; Eccl. 12:13). But because some people are yet to accept this truth, the devil uses them to oppose those who devote themselves to Christ (John 15:18-21). You have the right to your own convictions and owe no one an apology for believing the Truth. When you feel remorseful for pleasing God, it is the same thing as apologizing to the devil for obeying God and promising not to do it anymore. Fear will grip you if you bow to intimidation. And in no time, you will experience confusion, sadness, and then find no joy in obeying God.

If you do not recondition your mind immediately by rejoicing even when some people are angry with you, you will drift towards the world and become indifferent to the morality of God. *Therefore, to him who knows to do good and does not do it, to him it is sin* (James 4:17). To avoid backsliding, say 'No' to ungodliness without feeling guilty. Refuse to be coerced into apology whenever you do nothing wrong before God and man, no matter how much the devil accuses you through any person or your own mind.

God created you for His pleasure, not for anyone else's–including yourself (Is. 43:21; cf. Ps. 100:3). Whoever fights you while you do His will fights not you, but Him. As no one can defeat Him, you remain indomitable as long as you stand your ground in Him (Acts 5:39; 9:4-5; cf. Esth. 6:13). He has fortified you against the fear and intimidation of your adversaries before they show up. It is your responsibility not to cower because He who is in you is greater than he who is in them (1 John 4:4). Hear God's voice in His Word below.

*And thou, son of man, be not afraid of them, neither be afraid of their **words**, though briers and thorns be with thee, and thou dost dwell among scorpions: be not afraid of their words, nor be dismayed at their **looks**, though they be a rebellious house. Behold I have made **thy face strong against their faces**, and **thy forehead strong against their foreheads**. As an adamant harder than flint have I made thy forehead: **fear them not**, neither be dismayed at their looks... (Ezek. 2:6; 3:8-9). And they shall fight against thee; but they **shall not prevail** against thee; for **I am with thee**, saith the LORD, to deliver thee (Jer. 1:19).*

You feed people's ego when you submit to their intimidation, and thus make them appear more powerful than God. Your courage to continue in the will of God despite their harassments and threats will deflate their ego, enabling them to know they are dust, powerless and nothing. Their findings may humble them to accept Jesus as their Savior and submit to His Lordship. *...All flesh is **grass**, And all its loveliness is like the flower of the field. The grass **withers**, the flower **fades**, But the **word of our God stands forever**.*

> **Human beings are less than nothing before God.**

*Behold, the nations are as a drop in a bucket ... as the small dust on the scales... All nations before him are as nothing; and they are counted to him **less than nothing**, and **vanity** (Is. 40:6, 8, 15, 17).*

You may ask, 'How do I know with all certainty that I'm not guilty of someone's accusation'? According to Psalm (85:10), *righteousness and peace kiss each other*. This means righteousness brings forth peace. Peace is divine. You have indescribable peace and unwavering confidence when your deeds please God (Phil. 4:7; John 14:27; cf. Prov. 16:7).

*And the work of righteousness shall be **peace;** and the effect of righteousness **quietness** and **assurance** for ever* (Is. 32:17). God is just, and no one mocks Him; you cannot have His peace when

> **Guilt tag is in the offender's heart.**

you displease Him (Gal. 6:7; 1 John 3:20). There might be no physical tag on people who do wrong, but deep down in their hearts lay the guilt of sin, which makes peace, tranquility, and divine assurance impossible.

Someone may say, 'But this is stubbornness. How can one person be right against the majority'? Numbers are inconsequential in the battle of faith; what matters is God's presence and approval (1 Sam. 14:6, 10, 12-13). Anyone who insists on God's will has God's backing, although he may score low in human opinion polls.

The saying 'majority carries the vote' only counts with humans. With God, 'minority can win the case'. *What can we say to these things? If God be for us, who can be against us* (Rom. 8:31)? God does not need an opinion poll to determine any case, and accordingly warns His children against following the crowd. *You shall not follow a crowd to do evil; nor shall you testify in a dispute so as to turn aside after many to pervert justice* (Ex. 23:2).

Stubbornness insists on a purpose. At the circumcision of John the Baptist, his relatives named him Zacharias, but his mother disagreed with them and called him John. The confirmation of the name by her husband, Zacharias, who was dumb as a sign for the birth of the child proved Elizabeth was not wrong, although their relatives could regard her as being stubborn just for insisting on God's inspiration (Luke 1:59-63).

Zacharias, who became dumb while on his priestly duty, did not reveal the name to his wife before the birth of the child (Luke 1:11-13, 18, 20). But God, who is not an author of confusion and does not concur with human wisdom, laid the name in the spirit of Zacharias' wife so that there would be an agreement between them and His purpose.

Again, what shall we say of Noah, who stood with God against all the people living in his generation (Gen. 6:9; Heb. 11:7)? What about the prophet Micaiah, who alone told King Ahab the truth against four hundred prophets who prophesied lies to him (2 Chr. 18:5, 10-13,15-16, 22)? All these and many more should be eye-openers to us so that we do not succumb to 'majority syndrome' because we want to avoid being labeled stubborn.

Our faith must be forceful if we are to establish the will of God on earth. Any Christian who waits for the approval of men to obey God may wait in vain. *And from the days of John the Baptist until now the kingdom of heaven suffers violence, and the violent take it by force* (Matt. 11:12). It is the spiritually violent, not the cowardly, that can resist the intimidation of the ungodly and accomplish the purpose of God.

> **Spiritual violence targets devils, physical violence targets men.**

Having explained that refusal to be sorry for righteous deeds is stubbornness in a positive dimension, let us cite some biblical examples to buttress our claim. While John was in prison, he sent his disciples to confirm from Jesus whether He was the Messiah (Mark 6:17-18; Luke 7:18-19). Jesus did not answer the question, but told them to inform John about the mighty works of God which they saw. Immediately after this response Jesus said: *And blessed is he, whosoever shall not be offended because of me* (Luke 7:23).

As the forerunner of Jesus, John might have expected Jesus to secure his release, or at least visit him. But He did neither! Humanly speaking, John's expectation was in order since God promised to save His people through Jesus. If Jesus were truly the One whom John had been advertising His arrival, he, the forerunner, should be the first partaker of His goodness (2 Tim. 2:16)!

The Man he labored for all his life rather met him with what some of us may label an 'unconcerned attitude' (John 1:23, 27). Jesus came to please God, not man or Himself (John 4:34), the same way He saved us not to live for ourselves or others but Him (2 Cor. 5:15). If God had wanted Jesus to deliver John from the prison or visit him, He definitely would have done that. But God wanted neither; John had finished his ministry, and it pleased God to take him home that way.

Jesus was not sorry for His failure to visit or bail John. Therefore, saying...*blessed is he, whosoever shall not be offended because of me* is like saying, 'Blessed is anyone who accepts the way God handles any matter; blessed is anyone who disregards his feelings and views and believes God is good and just in whatever He does (Ps. 145:17); blessed is anyone who does not regret but rejoices when he obeys God; blessed is anyone who does not get angry because of the truth.'

> **Jesus was and is unapologetic and will never be apologetic.**

Jesus never apologized to any person for obeying God or speaking the truth; and we must imitate Him, just as the apostles did! When the Sadducees warned them not to preach in the name of Jesus, they continued to preach Christ, regardless. They got caught again and faced the elders of the synagogue. Instead of apologizing for disobeying their command, they said, ...*We ought to obey God rather than men* (Acts 5:29).

> **You are solid in Christ.**

Love every human being and give them their due respect, but do not fear them for any reason. It is fear that will make you accept their accusations and apologize. Being unapologetic about righteous and holy deeds is the way to maintain one's peace and joy, even back in the Old Testament. King David did not let his wife spoil his elated mood resulting from the successful transport of the Ark of God back to Jerusalem. His wife Michal, whose father, Saul, was the former king, despised and confronted him because he leaped and whirled before the LORD, but David did not say, 'Darling, I'm sorry for disgracing myself before my subjects today. I will be cautious about my dance next time, however joyful I am. It was a mistake. I promise to never act that way again. Please forgive me'. Rather, he replied to the wife with an unequivocal voice, as shown below.

*...It was **before the LORD**, who chose me instead of your father and all his house, to appoint me ruler over the people of the LORD, over Israel. Therefore I will **play music before the LORD**. And I will be even **more undignified** than this, and will be **humble in my sight**. But as for the maidservants of whom you have spoken, **by them I will be held in honor** (2 Sam. 6:21-22).*

Moreover, Mordecai never felt sorry for his refusal to bow to Haman, but cried bitterly to God for deliverance when Haman plot to kill all the Jews because of him (Esther 3:8-9; 4:1). Shadrach, Meshach, and Abed-nego did not apologize to King Nebuchadnezzar for spurning his idol, but on the contrary responded: *O Nebuchadnezzar, we are not careful to answer you in this matter* (Dan. 3:16). Daniel made himself available as meat for lions rather than regret his action, by defying King Darius' law of *'no prayer to any god or man except the king for thirty days'* (Dan. 6:7, 10, 16-17).

> **Say NO without feeling guilty.**

Disobedience is not an option to consider when the subject at hand involves God. Whatever the case, it certainly is not worth giving a thought to; therefore, maintain your integrity when you have obeyed God. People who disobey God are to repent, apologize to God, and join you to worship Him. You are not the one who should disobey God and join them in displeasing Him. Learn from God's counsel to Jeremiah: ... *Let them return to you, But you must not return to them* (Jer. 15:19).

My beloved friend, never feel guilty for obeying God, no matter what you are to face or already facing because of it. Such a feeling is the devil's seed of backsliding. You will become indifferent to righteous and holy living if you give in to it. It will benefit you to root out the seed of regret now if already sown, and make a habit of rejoicing always. Let your poise signal to your accusers that your obedience to God's righteous and holy ways is non-negotiable.

> **Obedience is way better than any sacrifice. Stick to obedience!**

Chapter Thirteen

KEEPING THE RIGHT COMPANIONS

Be not deceived: evil communications corrupt good manners (I Cor. 15:33).

The Bible encourages friendships but states clearly that bad associations will ruin one's life. *He that walketh with wise men shall be wise: but a companion of fools shall be destroyed* (Prov. 13:20). *Two are better than one, Because they have a good reward for their labour. For if they fall, one will lift up his companion. But woe to him who is alone when he falls, For he has no one to help him up. Another may overpower though, two can withstand him. And a threefold cord is not quickly broken* (Eccl. 4:9-10, 12; cf. Lev. 26:8).

The above Scriptures show that there is great power and strength in synergy. People have much more strength and influence when they put resources together and work in unity. A tree does not make a forest; you need like-minded people for greater heights–you need friends.

Friends are soul-mates who support one another at all costs and against all odds (1 Sam. 18:3; 20:1-17, 27-42; 2 Sam.1:25-26; 9:1). If you carefully read these reference Scriptures, you will observe there

> **True friendship is selfless.**

is indeed no selfishness in genuine friendship. If genuine friendships exist, then false friendships do too.

Let God guide you in choosing friends to avoid falling into the hands of religious fraudsters who take advantage of the believers' love. Discern the people you associate with even among believers, for the devil uses infiltration and imitation to wage war against the church of Christ (Gal. 2:4).

False brethren who are his servants do not come looking like wolves but like sheep, as Satan himself appears not as an angel of darkness, but an angel of light (Matt. 7:15; 2 Cor. 11:13-14).

> *Ignorant Christians are gullible.*

False Christians abuse love and take advantage of true but naive Christians (Jude 4, 12; 2 Pet. 2:18; 2 Tim. 3:5-7). Relationships with people of evil intentions are toxic and unsafe.

In making a choice of friends, avoid hypocrites–they are 'false-nice' people. Be careful of people who are overly pleasing or overly critical. Watch out for secretive people—they feign concern to invade your world but will not be open to you about their own lives: do not take them as confidants. *Faithful are the wounds of a friend, but the kisses of an enemy are deceitful* (Prov. 27:6).

We fall for phonies (deceivers), when we believe their words without verifying from the Lord (Josh. 9:3-9, 14-16; cf. 2 Cor. 5:16a). However, their insincerity always becomes glaring (Josh. 9:16; Col. 4:14b; cf. 2 Tim. 4:10a). Once you are aware of the deceiver, seek the mercy and counsel of God and separate yourself from him (2 Tim. 3:5; 2 Thess. 3:6; 1 Cor. 5:11).

In addition, pick lessons while you move forward. Every experience is for your spiritual training and maturity if you take advantage of it. Age does not make one spiritually or emotionally mature - experience and knowledge do. But sympathy seekers rarely learn from failed relationships; they like to hear only what they want. For this reason, they keep rotating from one false friend to another, who adds no value to their lives but only flatters and drains them.

> *Learn valuable lessons than mere regret when defrauded.*

A good friend is objective and will not indulge you, but with your cooperation, turn a devastating situation into an asset. *For by wise counsel you will wage your own war, And in multitude of counsellors there is safety* (Prov. 24:6). Any friend who dissuades you from carrying out a

> *True friends don't support childishness.*

difficult godly task for whatever reason does no good for you but for the devil (Matt. 16:21-23).

In addition, friends who condemn you rather than console you in the face of suffering arising because of your faithfulness to God are *forgers of lies* and *physicians of no value; miserable comforters* (Job 13:4; 16:2). The words of such 'friends' leave you confused, dejected, and weak if you assimilate them and will eventually kill your faith in God if you do not eject them.

In friendships, everybody is important and has something to offer. *As iron sharpens iron, So a man sharpens the countenance of his friend* (Prov. 27:17). Therefore, friendship with people of a different value system is not advisable (2 Cor. 6:14). It is fraught with misperception, dissension, suspicion, gossip, pretense, infighting, 'snail movement', or regression. You cannot progress in such a relationship, no matter how friendly you are, and it will surely break up because of dissension (heart disconnection).

To tie yourself with people whose mindsets differ from yours will leave you both weary and hurt because of friction—you try to pull them up and they attempt to drag you down. Eagles and fowls cannot fly together, although they are birds. Eagle flies high in the sky while fowl hops and flaps, remaining on the ground. *Can two walk together, unless they are agreed* (Amos 3:3)?

> **Eagle and fowl can't fly together.**

Friends are to be open to each other if they are to experience real fellowship. It is easier to talk about our accomplishments and the good sides of us than to expose the pale sides. Yet, true friendship occurs when the people involved are courageous and humble enough to share not only their joys but also their hurts, fears, weaknesses, and failures.

> **True friends share both joy and pain.**

A true friend holds back no useful information from his friend (John 15:15b; Acts 20:20). Friends feel relaxed and stick to self-control rather than seeking to control others when there is love, tolerance, endurance, care, forgiveness, and prayer of faith. Someone who controls his own spirit is mightier than the one who captures a city but fails in self-control (Prov. 16:32). Families where the members are friends to one another enjoy a closer bond.

Your choice of friends as a Christian should be people with similar interests: people who prioritize their relationship with Christ and are heavenly-minded (Phil. 4:3). It is among groups of Christians of active faith that members can stir up love and good works in one another. From here, you can draw encouragement to continue in the good fight of faith (Heb. 10:24-25; 1 Tim. 6:12).

Let Jesus as your first Friend help you make the right friends.

Friends who inspire you to actualize God's eternal purpose for your life are your greatest assets on earth.

Chapter Fourteen

HOLDING YOU RESPONSIBLE

...Be fruitful, and multiply, and replenish the earth, and subdue it: and have dominion... (Gen. 1:27).

Everyone wants a solution to their problem and most people think they can get solutions by merely telling others about their problems. You are the center of your life and it is your primary duty to care for every part of you: your spirit, soul, and body. You are unique, and the best person to handle you is you.

No one (including God) can help you get out of your problem without you resisting forces that will deter you from being totally committed to the actions necessary for the solution (John 5:8-11; cf. James 4:7). Deeper revelations and quiet confidence result from obedience (John 5:12-15; cf. John 9:7, 9, 25, 35-38).

> **God is ever ready to help you if you are willing.**

You will labor in vain if your field is wasting away, while you choose to impress others by taking up their responsibilities. *Look not upon me, because I am black, because the sun hath looked upon me: my mother's children were angry with me; they made me the keeper of the vineyards;* **but mine own vineyard have I not kept** (Song 1:6).

Personal success eludes us when we are lazy or working foolishly, not knowing how to balance personal and group activities. *He who tilleth his land shall have plenty of bread: but he that followeth after vain persons shall have poverty enough* (Prov. 28:19). However hard you work in a group, you cannot stand out when you are not an authority in your domain. A tree without fruits does not attract attention, even

> **Your offer is as weighty as your worth.**

if it provides shade. Fruits make a tree noticeable. Develop your gift(s) so you can render honorable service. *Seest thou a man diligent in his business? he shall stand before kings; he shall not stand before mean men* (Prov. 22:29; cf. 2 Tim. 2:20-21).

The results of personal negligence include confusion, defeat, failure, and poverty; not just monetary, but in mentality and skills. We often ignore our foolish ways that make us unsuccessful and become angry even with God, who has already blessed and endowed us with everything it takes to rule the earth as shown in our opening Scripture (Gen. 1:27). *The foolishness of man twists his way, And his heart frets against the LORD* (Prov. 19:3).

Daily choices are significant to victory: we permit whatever happens to us by the choices we make. You are to hold yourself responsible for personal progress; blaming others, God, or the devil will not solve the problem of personal regression. Regardless of what others are to you, you still need to be YOU and be a friend of YOU to encourage or restrain YOU.

> **Self is the problem: examine you.**

Being yourself in a relationship does not mean being self-centered. Instead, it means holding on to your conviction with a clear conscience based on your personal trust in God, for *the just shall live by **his** faith* (Hab. 2:4; cf. 1 Cor. 16:12; Rom. 14:5b). Therefore, do not lose your very person to the friendship of your fellow humans as good and strong as the relationship is or else it becomes idolatry. If you can relate well with yourself, you discover that self can be a major obstacle or catalyst to progress. You will hardly understand others or relate well with them when you do not understand yourself.

Nobody (including Satan) is any other person's problem: each person is his own problem (John 3:17-21). Satan and his agents can never overcome you in any battle unless you relinquish your power and cooperate with them. *We know that whoever is born of God sinneth not; but he that is begotten of God keepeth himself, and that **wicked one toucheth him not*** (1 John 5:18).

> **No entity can defeat you if you don't help them.**

To be friendly with YOU means:

- That you do not indulge or hate, but love yourself instead, for you can only love others as you love yourself. *...You shall love your neighbour as yourself* (Matt. 22:39). To love oneself is to serve others delightfully and not being selfish; selfishness ruins all relationships. If you harm yourself, you will definitely harm your neighbors instead of loving them.

- That you do not crowd yourself with activities such that you have little or no time for yourself.

- That you do not have unreasonable expectations of yourself, but learn from your mistakes and proceed.

- That you do not let people or circumstances determine your divine assignment; let God relate to you personally. Labor spiritually according to the gift of God in you; it is your responsibility to begin (2 Tim. 1:6, 9; cf. Matt. 25:24-30). Ask God the right question, like Saul, if you are confused about your role. ... *Lord, **what** wilt thou have me to do* (Acts 9:6)?

- That you know who you are (Matt. 16:13-17). You are not who you think you are or who people say you are, but who God says you are. God is the One that defines you and He says you are *fearfully and wonderfully made* in all aspects (Ps. 139:14). **Your victory in life starts with the acceptance of your identity in God but the hardest work you do on earth is to resist all oppositions whether subtle or apparent, to become who you ought to be** (cf. 1 Sam. 17:26-30, 31-37, 40, 49-50, 56, 2 Sam.5:4-5).

- That you do not look down on or write yourself off. The way you perceive yourself affects you far more than the opinions people form about you. Your thoughts attract who or what comes to you.

- That you do not be a hypocrite, justifying yourself for the same behavior you condemn in others. Correct yourself before you correct others (Matt. 7:5).

- That you pursue God and not men for sufficiency. You will be depressed if you go after men. *All the brothers of the poor hate him; How much more do his friends go far from him! He may pursue them with words, yet they abandon him* (Prov. 19:7).

- That you do not engage in group work and neglect your personal work–ensure you do that which no other person can do but you, and then contribute your quota in a group activity.

- That you attempt not to be like another person but to be true to yourself. You feel fulfilled when you are you. In addition, respect yourself - when you respect yourself, you do not demand respect from others but your character commands it of them. You do not force respect but earn it.

- That you cry when you must; it is all part of a healing process. But never pity yourself or seek the sympathy of others–it will make you have a *'poor me'* mentality. People with such mindsets relentlessly seek human approval and are blind to opportunities. They are never victorious.

- That you do not imagine or say negative things that can keep you from forward and upward movements. In all situations, believe and say, *I can do all things through Christ who strengthens me* for the grace of God is perfect when you are weak (Phil. 4:13; 2 Cor. 12:9).

- That you do not compare yourself to any person but appreciate *you* and other people. It is unwise to compare yourself to others (2 Cor. 10:12). Such comparison is an evil seed that sprouts the feeling of superiority or inferiority; superiority when you feel you are better than them, and inferiority when you feel they are better than you. These feelings are vices and neither is better than the other. Everyone is unique; value you and others (cf. Phil. 2:3-4).

- That you do not compete, but cooperate with others when necessary. You were born alone, and you will die alone. To compete with others is to distract yourself from your divine purpose and thus, lose divine direction. Intra-competition drives you to your goal; while extra-competitions will engross you in a rat race. Compete with no one but yourself.

- That you compare *you* to only *you*. Assess your previous performance, compare it with the present, and strive to perform better. *But let each one examine his own work, and then he will have rejoicing in himself alone, and not in another. For each one shall bear his own load* (Gal. 6:4-5).

- That you do not commit yourself to people, or else their unreliability will crush your heart. *The heart is deceitful above all things, and desperately wicked: who can know it* (Jer. 17:9)? Do good to people, but commit yourself to God. Jesus did not commit Himself to people, although He performed various miracles for them; His unalloyed devotion was to God alone (John 2:23-25; 4:34). To commit yourself to God is to deny yourself: to surrender your ambitions, will, intellect, emotions, and all you have to Christ. He will never shortchange you; He will give you the best instead.

- That you do not trade your soul for the things of this world. You brought nothing into this world and will carry nothing to your grave (Eccl. 5:15). Learn from the dead while you live (Eccl. 7:2, 4), and do not play with sin as it will emasculate and enslave you (Rom. 6:16; cf. John 8:34).

If you can relate well with yourself, you will find out that self-control is the key to a calm environment. It enables you to make adjustments from your end, by which you avoid bickering with others and allow them their freedom. *And just as you want men to do to you, you also do to them likewise* (Luke 6:31).

You relate to people not as they are but as you are when you have self-control, thus imparting moral conduct to them. *Most assuredly, I say to you, unless a grain of wheat falls into the ground and dies, it remains alone; but if it dies, it produces much grain* (John 12:24).

Having discussed friendship with others and yourself, it is important to note that both you and others can fail *you*. You may try hard to help yourself, but fail. Friends might surround you, but be spiritually unavailable and unhelpful because of their own distresses or inability. Jesus Christ is the only Companion that does not fail and He is the source of true companionship. He alone is always present, available, and helpful (Matt.28:20). He *loveth at all times and sticketh closer than a brother* (Prov. 17:17; 18:24).

> **Jesus is the main Friend; put your whole trust in Him.**

The case of a man with an infirmity for thirty-eight years is a good example of how all humans (including ourselves) can disappoint us. His family and friends abandoned him, and he tried in vain to help himself. Only Jesus cared and cured him (John 5:5-9). You dare not trust in yourself or any other person but God.

Thus saith the LORD; Cursed be the man that trusteth in man, and maketh the flesh his arm, and whose heart departeth from the LORD. Blessed is the man that trusteth in the LORD, and whose hope the LORD is (Jer. 17:5, 7).

Chapter Fifteen

OPERATE FROM THE VICTORY POINT

...Pursue, for you shall surely overtake them and without fail recover all
(I Sam. 30:8).

Y**ou** need constant decisions and actions to get to a successful end. The challenge before you at every decision is the balancing of your feelings and thoughts so that you become neither an oppressor nor a victim. Any decision taken out of anger or bitterness is often subjective and on the wrong premises. Although it may appear right and promising at the beginning, in the long run, it disappoints. *There is a way which seemeth right unto a man, but the end thereof are the ways of death* (Prov. 14:12).

Our point of victory starts with making the right decisions. The impact of the decision made based on either feeling or thought cannot be the same as the one made based on the interaction of the two. Feelings may trigger reasoning or reasoning feelings, but both must work as a unit if we are to make informed decisions that bring desired results.

Let us expound this point with the incident in First Samuel (30:1-24). [Read it for better understanding.] Consider these verses below (1, 3-4, 6, 8).

*...Amalekites had invaded ... Ziklag... So David and his men came to the city, and, behold, it was burned with fire; and their wives, and their sons, and their daughters, were taken captive. Then David and the people that were with him **lifted up their voice and wept, until they had no more power to weep**. And **David** was **greatly distressed**; for the people spake of **stoning him**, because the **soul** of all the people was **grieved**, every man for his sons and for his daughters. But **David encouraged himself in the LORD his God**. And David **enquired at the LORD**, saying, Shall*

I pursue after this troop? shall I overtake them? And he answered him, **Pursue***, for thou shalt surely* **overtake** *them and without fail* **recover all***.*

David went to war with his army. On return, they discovered that the people of Amalek, an enemy tribe, had kidnapped their families and burned their city. The situation affected all of them, including their leader, David. He stood out as a victor because of his approach, not his position. Let us see how he handled the situation that led to his triumph (verses 4, 6, 8, 11-12, 16, 19-20, 22-24).

1. All of them felt bad and cried to the point of exhaustion, including David.

2. The men sank deeper into their emotions, this time passing blame. They wanted to stone David, feeling their trouble was his fault—I guess they thought they would have been home to defend their dependents if he had not taken them to war.

3. David let his mind have the upper hand over his emotions. Even though his trouble was now doubled–his kidnapped community plus displaced anger of his armies–he did not blame his army or seek their sympathy. Neither did he pity himself.

4. David arose from the shackles of feelings and encouraged himself in the LORD his God. The soul of David bowed to his spirit for his mind to receive strength from the Holy Spirit to seek a solution to the problem. *Why art thou cast down, O my* **soul***? And why art thou disquieted in me? Hope thou in God: for I shall yet praise him for the help of his countenance* (Ps. 42:5).

> **People who draw encouragement from God enjoy emotional stability.**

When we stay in our emotional zone longer than necessary, we might refuse encouragement from our spirit, and antagonize anyone who wants us to reason out the situation. We rather accept to be **victims**. As victims, we pamper our feelings, wallow in self-pity, seek sympathy, complain about the situation, blame people or circumstances, and live in false hope as we reject personal responsibility, which is very necessary if we must conquer.

5. David inquired from the Victor Himself–God. God instructed him on what to do. He acted quickly and caught the people in their merriment. Do not delay action when you receive instructions on what to do. *I made haste, and delayed not to keep thy commandment* (Ps. 119:60).

Delayed action is a loophole for unnecessary troubles that may either thwart or defeat a purpose. *He also that is slothful in his work is brother to him that is a great waster* (Prov. 18:9). An Igbo adage says, *'eme ngwa ngwa emeghara ọdachi'* [you avoid tragedy when you act fast.].

6. War preoccupied David's mind, but his emotions were equally active. That made him notice and resuscitate an abandoned Egyptian servant to an Amalekite, who gave him valuable information against his enemies. We miss significant benefits when we are insensitive to the needs of others or suffering people around us.

7. David recovered all they lost besides the spoils of the enemy. He who networks with God becomes a victor himself.

8. David was impartial. He prevented the feelings of pride and greed that would have made him lose the joy of victory.

The attitude of David towards his associates, both strong and weak, was proof his decisions were not out of resentment. He cared for all and treated them well. He was a **victor** indeed. A victor is unbiased and serves to the glory of God and for the benefit of all. He knows God raised him *for the sake of His people* (2 Sam. 5:12). If David had grudges against his associates, he would have seized the opportunity some of his men offered and caused division among the entire army. While the men fought one another and sought his favor, he could have played a righteous judge in pretense.

He could sit back and laugh at all of them, saying in his heart: 'You united against me, now fight and finish yourselves'. The schemes and the motives would qualify him as an **oppressor**. An oppressor is manipulative, vindictive, and delights in the plight of others.

We can slip from being victors to be oppressors if we are not watchful of our behavior (2 Chr. 14:2; cf. 16:10, 12; 26:3,5; cf. 16, 19). The devil always shows up whether in victory or defeat to lure us to either pride or shame. You increase in humility if every situation draws you closer to God, but become overtaken by pride if they drive you away from Him.

> *One can start a task in humility and end in pride; put your motive in check.*

Therefore, whether you eat or drink, or whatever you do, do all to the glory of God (1 Cor. 10:31). David would have sabotaged the goodness of God if he had not acknowledged God for their victory or if he had sidelined the weak men in his army. The victory which ought to bring joy to the entire community would have resulted in division, jealousy, and a senseless war between the oppressors and the victims. Negative emotions such as pride, shame, greed, and jealousy give the devil a chance to operate freely in people, using them to ruin their lives and society.

The tragedy of a 'feel good mentality'

We need to note the effect of pleasure without caution. The Amalekites were celebrating their great booty–eating, drinking, and dancing–and were unobservant at the insecurity in their city. Verse seventeen says that *David smote them from the twilight even unto the evening of the next day: and there escaped not a man of them, save four hundred young men...*

This shows they were in a drunken stupor, a state that is triggered and maintained by a 'feel good mentality'. A situation where people isolate their minds from their emotions and live by feelings alone is appalling. Such people wallow in ignorance and are bad influences because they lack not only the knowledge but also the understanding of the times.

We must harness the messages of our mind [= I think] and emotion [= I feel] to take the right decision and action at every point in time for victory. David would have missed vital information that helped him strategize for war against the Amalekites if he had ignored his feelings and overlooked the anguish of the abandoned Amalekite servant.

The four hundred men of Amalek who escaped the sword of David were on guard while they feasted - their feelings were in check by their thoughts. They parallel the five proverbial wise virgins who had extra oil in their lamps that enabled their readiness at the bridegroom (Matt. 25:4, 9-10). People who misuse time feel they have enough time to do anything they want. However, we all, as stewards of time, have a brief time on earth to finish the work God assigned us for His praise (Is. 43:21).

Understanding the fleeting nature of time is crucial if we are to be truly successful; otherwise, we will waste our time on frivolities and miss opportunities. Moses, the humblest servant of God (Num. 12:3), knew the shortness of time on earth and prayed for wisdom to manage it well. *So teach us to number our days, that we may apply our hearts unto wisdom* (Ps. 90:12). The children of Issachar understood the significance of time and were prompt in their dealings. *And the children of Issachar, which were men that had understanding of times, to know what Israel ought to do…* (1 Chr. 12:32).

Let us admit our ignorance and misuse of time and cry to God for mercy and understanding, so we can become good managers of time for the remaining fraction of our time here on earth. As the Amalekites were wining and dining, oblivious to their sudden destruction, so are most people in our society today living in utter ignorance of the impending devastation of the world. *The earth is the LORD's* and He determines its timetable (Ps. 24:1; 1 Chr. 16:26; Ps. 115:3).

Our Lord Jesus Christ did not leave us uninformed of His second coming on the earth, the events preceding it, and the escape route (Matt. 24; cf. Luke 21). Adherence to His and other biblical preventive counseling and total reliance on the Holy Spirit's leadership for eternal safety is the only sure way to overcome the dangers of the last days.

For as many as are led by the Spirit of God, they are the sons of God. Nay, in all these things we are more than conquerors through him that loved us (Rom. 8:14, 37). *…having believed, you were sealed with the Holy Spirit of promise, who is the guarantee of our inheritance until the redemption of the possessed possession to the praise of His glory* (Eph. 1:13-14).

But take heed to yourselves, lest your hearts be weighed down with carousing, drunkenness, and cares of this life, and that Day come on you unexpectedly. For it will come as a snare on all those who dwell on the face of the whole earth. Watch therefore, and pray always that you may be counted worthy to escape all these things that will come to pass, and to stand before the Son of Man (Luke 21:34-36).

For when they say, "Peace and safety!" then sudden destruction comes upon them, as labor pains upon a pregnant woman. And they **shall not escape** (1 Thess. 5:3).

Chapter Sixteen

BE A GIVER

...it is more blessed to give than to receive (Acts 20:35).

Whenever giving is mentioned, most people's minds run to money. While some are ready to give, others think they have nothing to give. The story of the widow's two mites shows that money is the least gift and everyone can give it (Mark 12:41-44). Giving is not robbery or cheating–it is not robbing Peter to pay Paul (2 Cor. 8:13). It is not a payment of tax.

Giving is an act of charity that you do willingly, cheerfully, proportionately, and sacrificially (Ex. 35:5, 22b-23a; 1 Cor. 8:3, 5, 12, 14-15). You do not borrow to give or give grudgingly (2 Cor. 8:12-13; 9:7). You give out of what you have as the Holy Spirit stirs up your spirit (Ex. 35:21a). You give by choice, not out of coercion or manipulation.

God has given us wonderful gifts of words, time, energy (John 17:8a; Acts 3:6), and much more which do not require money to share. All we need to be is selfless to use them in proper service to others. What words do you share with people: lies or truth, encouraging or discouraging words, constructive or destructive words (John 17:17; Prov. 18:21)?

How much valuable time do you share with others, beginning with your conjugal family? How much of your energy do you give in the serve to others: do you spend your strength only when you will get rewards? Can you run errands without desiring compensation? How do you expect to receive without giving?

Some Christians complain about the rich who are stingy, and hardly recognize that they, too, are misers. How does a Christian who withholds the gospel of salvation from the sinful and hungry souls differ from someone who is stingy with money? Is he not more wicked, seeing that what he refuses to share is of eternal value? How is a Christian who does not give quality time better than a person who refuses to give financial help? How does a Christian who abuses the grace of God differ from someone who misuses money?

We harden our conscience the more when we justify our omissions and find faults with others (Rom. 2:21-24). We must deal with our own faults before we can correctly help others with theirs (Matt. 7:5). When we do what God expects of us, compassion will move us to intercede before Him for people who do things their own way, knowing that everyone is accountable to God (Rom. 14:12).

Samuel did not support Israel when they rejected God as their King, but he prayed for them, nonetheless. *Moreover God forbid that I should sin against the LORD in ceasing to pray for you...* (1 Sam. 12:23). His statement implies that prayer of intercession is giving and failure to do so is selfish and sinful. An intercessor spends his intimate fellowship with God, pleading for others. Do you genuinely seek God in prayer on behalf of other people? If yes, you are performing an act of giving.

The church of Christ is languishing, and the world is perishing, because of the spiritual laziness and insensitivity of Christians who give nothing. They hide or hoard their gifts, or use them for bullying and/or self-indulgence (Matt. 25:25-26; 24:49). *The liberal soul shall be made fat... He that withholdeth corn, the people shall curse him...* and God will eternally punish him if he does not repent (Prov. 11:25-26; cf. Matt. 25:28-30; Num. 32:20-23).

In effect, everyone has something to give, including money (1 Cor. 12:7; Eph. 4:7; cf. 2 Cor. 8:14). No matter your difficulty or how little you have to spare, giving is inexcusable (2 Cor. 8:2, 5; cf. Matt. 25:24, 27-28). If you do not give out of inconvenience or out of the little you have, you will not give even in comfort or much (Luke 16:10). It is not the amount that determines the value of a gift, but what it costs the giver (2 Samuel. 24:24; Mark 12:41-44).

Someone with a greedy heart does not really give. He makes a show of giving to achieve his selfish intent. Such giving is bribery and brings God no glory and has no eternal reward (Matt. 6:1-2).

Every disciple of Christ is working in the 'Delivery Department of Christ's Kingdom [DDCK]'. Christ called, chose, employed, and anointed us to distribute His products to people (John 15:16). These products are both spiritual and material. Some Christians are stingy and hoard the products for themselves and their families. Some are covetous: they only distribute the products to make merchandise of the recipients. Some are wicked and lazy; they sit on the products and give excuses (Matt. 25:24-26).

These conducts contradict the Producer's instruction: *...freely ye have received, freely give* (Matt. 10:8). We will give freely and to the pleasure of God when we recognize that all we have is from God and for Him, and appreciate our position as stewards (John 3:27; 1 Cor. 4:7; Hag. 2:8). As the elders in heaven say, *Thou art worthy, O Lord, to receive glory and honour and power: for thou hast created all things, and for thy pleasure they are and were created* (Rev. 4:11), let the saints on the earth say, 'Amen' and translate the Word into action.

Recall the action of David in chapter fifteen - how he erased greed with the law of giving which he proved by sending portions of the spoil to the elders in his homeland, his friends, and acquaintances in various places (1 Sam. 30:26-31). His remark in verse twenty-six to the recipients is insightful - *...Here is a present for you from the spoil of the enemies of the LORD.*

David directly linked the enemies to God and not to himself. If the enemies are God's enemies, then the spoil is also God's spoil. David is simply the distributor, giving others their portion and taking his. Our riches and gifts will be of eternal joy if we refuse to put our trust in them, but willingly and readily use them for good works and promotion of the gospel of Christ (1 Tim. 6:10, 17-19).

Stinginess is corruption, just like greed (Prov. 11:26a; Is. 56:11). Holiness requires that you do not withhold the good you are to release to others or covet other people's possessions (Ex. 20:17), instead of that, bless others as God blesses you, whether with spiritual or material things.

> *A stingy person is as corrupt as the greedy.*

While you perform an act of charity, ensure your confidence is in God who alone is good and not in self-righteousness, which is as a filthy rag before God (Matt. 19:17; Is. 64:6).

Trust in the LORD, and do good... (Ps. 37:3). Trust, apart from being the foundation of your relationship with God, strengthens your heart to continue doing good, even when you encounter wicked recipients who pay back good with evil (Is. 26:10). Trusting in yourself will lead to disappointment and discouragement, making you become absolutely insensitive to the needs of others.

However, the essence of giving is not for self-glorification but to show the kindness of God, our heavenly Father, who is generous both to the righteous and the wicked (Matt. 5:44-45). We will overcome the temptation of insensitivity to human welfare, particularly to the ingrates if our focus is not on benefits to self, but to glorifying God. Let the driving force for your act of giving be God's reward and not the accolades of men. You will lose eternal benefits if you insist on people's appreciation (Matt. 6:1-4).

> **Give out of compassion whether to the good or to the wicked.**

Remember, *it is more blessed to give than to receive* (Acts 20:35). Giving is both a choice and a privilege. Do it freely and expect nothing from the recipients (not even a 'thank you') so that negative responses will not affect you. The return of ingratitude for kindness is the devil's trick to make you selfish and to stop giving. And by so doing, you block the conduit to your blessings. Your reward comes from God, whom you obey (Luke 6:35), so give regardless.

> **You are more blessed giving than receiving.**

You will maintain your blessings and prosper more and more if you continue to give (Gal. 6:9). Take these Scriptures to heart. *Give, and it shall be given to you: good measure, pressed down, shaken together, and running over will be put into your bosom. For with the same measure that you use, it will be measured back to you* (Luke 6:38). *And let us not be weary in well doing: for in due season we shall reap, if we faint not* (Gal. 6:9).

Chapter Seventeen

SILENCE

He who guards his mouth preserves his life, but he who opens wide his lips shall have destruction (Prov. 13:3).

Be quiet when necessary and watch events as they unfold. You do not have to respond to every question or question every situation. Keeping mute at appropriate times is a victory on its own. God commands us to be fast hearers and slow speakers (James 1:19). Perhaps that is why He designed two ears and one mouth.

> **Silence gives opportunity for proper observation.**

Let us learn from our Lord Jesus, who sometimes refrained from providing answers to the questions posed to Him. Consider these Scriptures:

And while He [Jesus] *was being accused by the chief priests and elders, He answered **nothing**. Then Pilate says to Him, "Do You not hear how many things they testify against You?" But He answers him **not one word**, so that the governor marvelled greatly (Matt. 27:12-14). Then he* (Herod) *questioned Him with many words, but He answered him **nothing*** (Luke 23:9). *Therefore… Pilate… went again into the Praetorium, and says to Jesus, "Where are You from?" But Jesus gave him **no answer*** (John 19:8-9).

Jesus promised that the Holy Spirit will speak through us when anyone interrogates us (Matt. 10:18-20; Luke 12:11-12). Do not say a word except the Holy Spirit prompts you to speak in any issue; otherwise, your words will ensnare you. Whenever someone is questioning you, pay close attention to your spirit and discern whether to respond. You may sometimes observe that you lack words to express yourself despite your willingness to do so. Under

> **Being unassertive at the right time is wisdom.**

such a circumstance, do not force yourself to speak or allow someone to put words in your mouth.

Accept to be unassertive. It pays to be dumb when the situation demands it than to be a parrot, proving your rights. *A fool's mouth is his destruction, and his lips are the snare of his soul* (Prov. 18:7). King David choose to be deaf and dumb at the moment of his trial than his enemies to trap him by his words. Observe his words in Psalms (38:12-14; 39:1-2).

*They also that seek after my life lay snares for me: and they that seek my hurt speak mischievous things, and imagine deceits all the day long. But I, as a **deaf** man, heard not; and I was as a **dumb** man that openeth not his mouth. Thus I was as a man that heareth not, and in whose mouth are no reproofs. I said, I will take heed to my ways, that I sin not with my tongue: I will keep my mouth with a bridle, while the wicked is before me. I was dumb with silence, I held my peace, even from good...*

King David could be silent before his enemies because he trusted God to help him and God indeed withheld him from speaking. *I was dumb, I opened not my mouth; because thou* [God] *didst it* (Ps. 39:9).

God will direct our speech by His Spirit if we submit to His guidance. To keep silent rather than assert yourself (especially when you are right), may seem foolish and cowardly in the sight of the world and carnal Christians. But to the spiritually mature, it is an express demonstration of wisdom and humility. There is certainly treasure in constructive silence.

> *Silence can be golden; practice it with God's intuition.*

Chapter Eighteen

HOPE AGAINST HOPE

Who against hope believed in hope... (Rom. 4:18).

There may be a period in one's life when it appears as if God is not responsive anymore; a time when it seems He is unconcerned about His child's condition. A time when one has prayed, fasted, obeyed, and manifested faith, labored in God's business, and done everything humanly necessary and possible, yet their predicament persists.

Jesus called such difficult times *the hour of the persecutors and the power of darkness* (Luke 22:53). It is an hour preceding great glory; an hour, God allows the enemy to do his worst and last battle, which cannot exceed the last minute of the hour. It is the time of great shaking that proves the persecuted really loves God and has faith in Him alone (John 14:30-31).

At such a time, many people (including carnal Christians) mock and doubt that person's sonship in God (Matt. 27:43). But after this dark hour comes the glorious morning; the time God turns around the situation in favor of the persecuted and glorifies His holy name. It is the time God derides His enemies by bestowing His glory on His persecuted child; the time He makes His child famous to bring more people to Himself.

They that sow in tears shall reap in joy. ...weeping may endure for a night, but joy cometh in the morning. And he has put a new song in my mouth, even praise unto our God: many shall see it, and fear, and shall trust in the LORD (Ps. 126:5; 30:5; 40:3).

Every suffering goes with shame, but ahead of it lies the glory (Luke 24:26; 1 Pet. 1:11b). To escape the shame is to miss the glory - the reason many Christians do not, and cannot, have notable success in their spiritual, social, and material lives. Only those who stand a particular trial to the end receive the blessings attached to it. *Blessed is the man who endures temptation; for when he has been approved, he will receive the crown of life which the Lord has promised to those who love him* (James 1:12). *But he that shall endure unto the end, the same shall be saved* (Matt. 24:13).

God is faithful to His promises and in control of the end from the beginning. He is with you, even in the most difficult time. God can sometimes be silent, yet His silence is not His absence. In His silence, He still feels your pain and directs the course of events to your good and victory (Is. 63:9; cf. Acts 9:4-5). His assurance to Israel when they complained of being deserted is the same for you. *But Zion said, The LORD hath forsaken me, and my Lord hath forgotten me. Can a woman forget her sucking child, that she should not have compassion on the son of her womb? yea, they may forget,* **yet will I not forget thee** (Is.49:14-15).

However, you need to be visionary to endure the shame of trials and inherit your wealth and eternal blessings at the end (Prov. 8:20-21; cf. Matt. 19:27-29). *"For your shame, I will give you double"*, says God to you (Is. 61:7). The life of Jesus shows us that humiliation is the way to exaltation, and that hope neglects the little gains of today for the great benefits of tomorrow (Heb. 12:2). Hope goes with contentment and prevents us from transacting our salvation for momentary pleasures like Esau, who sold his birthright for one morsel of food (Heb. 12:16).

> **Endure the shame to the end and get the glory at the end.**

People who lack vision waste their lives in superficialities and die with no eternal accomplishment (Prov. 29:18). Vision in this context is a revelation, an insight from God about the future (John 16:13; cf. Gen. 13:14-15; 15:13-14).

Naturally, Abraham had no hope of bearing the promised child with Sarah, yet he hoped. He was 99 years old when God reassured him of the birth of the covenant child (Gen. 17:1-2, 17). Sarah, his wife, delivered the promised child without health complications at a postmenopausal age of 90 while he was 100 (Gen. 18:12-14; cf. 21:5). Do not lose hope in whatever the unfailing God has promised you. Only unbelief can abort such promises (Heb. 3:19).

The grace to endure to the end is available in Jesus Christ: trust and abide in Him. *Looking unto Jesus the author and finisher of our faith; who for the joy that was set before him endured the cross, despising the shame, and is set down at the right hand of the throne of God* (Heb. 12:2).

Hope is *an anchor of the soul* (Heb. 6:19). The ultimate hope is not the hope for the end of any problem here in this world, but the hope for the end of your battle of faith - *the salvation of your soul* is the end *of your faith. Wherefore gird up the loins of your mind, be sober, and* **hope to the end** *for the grace that is* **to be brought** *unto you at the* **revelation of Jesus Christ** (1 Pet. 1:9 rephrased, 13). *For we are made partakers of Christ, if we hold* **the beginning** *of our confidence steadfast unto* **the end** (Heb. 3:14). *Cast not away therefore your confidence, which hath* **great recompence** *of reward* (Heb. 10:35).

Some of God's promises which we have received in faith may not manifest in our lifetime but in the lives of our descendants after we have gone to be with the Lord in heaven (Heb. 11:13). I appeal to you to study the life of our father in faith, Abraham, to have a good grasp of this truth.

However, do not trouble your mind figuring out which promise happens at what time. God does not make mistakes: He knows which and when; nobody gives Him counsel on what to do, and neither can anyone withhold His purpose from Him (Is. 40:14; Job 42:2).

Your offspring are a part of God's covenant with you. *This is my covenant with them, saith the LORD; My spirit that is upon thee, and my words which I have put in thy mouth, shall not depart out of thy mouth, nor out of the mouth of thy seed, nor out of the mouth of thy seed's seed, saith the LORD, from henceforth and for ever. ...I will pour my spirit upon thy seed, and my blessing upon thine offspring* (Is. 59:21; 44:3b).

You are still part of whatever blessings God passes to them. Consider further the following Scriptures.

...the mercy of the LORD is from everlasting to everlasting upon them that fear him, and his righteousness unto children's children (Ps. 103:17). *The children of thy servants shall continue, and their seed shall be established before thee* (Ps. 102:28).

Behold, I and the children whom the LORD hath given me are for signs and for wonders… (Is. 8:18). *For as the new heavens and the new earth, which I will make, shall remain before me, saith the LORD, so shall your seed and your name remain* (Is. 66:22). *For the unbelieving husband is sanctified by the wife, and the unbelieving wife is sanctified by the husband: else were your children unclean; but now **are they holy*** (1 Cor. 7:14).

Take these verses of the Bible to heart and relax in the love and faithfulness of God. All of God's promises in Christ are settled forever and they are not limited to you, but extended to your descendants, yet unborn. … *God is in the generation of the righteous* (Ps. 14:5). Importantly, the manifestations of the promises glorify the name of God and not your name, so their fulfillment is more significant to God than you, unless you are drawing attention to yourself, which is idolatry.

Hear it once again from the mouth of Mary, the wife of Joseph, whom the LORD favored to be the instrument for the virgin birth of our Lord Jesus Christ - …*his* [God's] *mercy is on them that fear him from generation to generation* (Luke 1:50).

Beloved friend, there is no controversy, for all God's promises are unchanging and fulfilled for us in Christ Jesus; Jesus is the answer to all our needs. *For all the promises of God in him* [Christ] *are yea, and in him* [Christ] *Amen, unto the glory of God…* (2 Cor. 1:20).

Chapter Nineteen

REJOICING ALWAYS

Rejoice in the Lord alway: and again I say, Rejoice (Phil. 4:4).

You need to keep hope alive as you wait for the manifestation of God's promises. *For hope saves us: but hope that is seen is not hope: for what a man seeth, why doth he yet hope for? But if we hope for that we see not, then do we with patience wait for it* (Rom. 8:24-25).

You have the right of inheritance in Christ (Rom. 8:17). God owns heaven and earth and has bequeathed everything to Christ (Matt. 11:27). *Therefore let no man boast in men. For all things are yours: And you are Christ's, and Christ is God's* (1 Cor. 3:21, 23).

You are already a winner! Your miracle is just in the womb of God's time, for there is nothing hard for God to do (Gen. 18:14). God's time is eternity, and He does not work according to man's limited time. So as the delivery lingers, you need strength for the waiting period. Your strength is tied to your joy - joy about what God has done, is doing, or yet to do. Your joy in God provides you with His strength to hang on until you receive what He promised you. *...the joy of the Lord is your strength* (Neh. 8:10d).

> *The joy of the Lord is your daily strength: taste and see.*

The fullness of joy is in the presence of God (Ps. 16:11). We live in God's presence when we abide in His Word and pray accordingly in every situation (John 15:7). Learn from the prophet Habakkuk who prays and rejoices in hope of God's mercy while his nation, Israel, bore the punishment of the sins of her people. Hear him:

A prayer of Habakkuk the prophet... Though the fig tree may not blossom, Nor fruit be on the vines; Though the labor of the olive may fail, And the fields yield no food; Though the flock may be cut off from the fold, And there be no herd in the stalls: **Yet I will rejoice in the LORD, I will joy in the God of my salvation. The LORD God is my strength;** *He will make* *my feet like deer's feet, And He will make me walk on my high hills* (Hab. 3:1, 17-19).

Do you know why Habakkuk made a choice to rejoice even when nothing good appears to be in sight? He knew in whom he believed - *the LORD God who is merciful and gracious, long suffering and abundant in goodness and truth* (Ex. 34:6), the God who cannot lie or say a thing without doing it, whose word is infallible, who honors His word above His name, who no one can set briers and thorns against in battle, the One who has the final say (2 Tim. 1:12; Num. 23:19; Ps. 138:2; Is. 27:4; Lam. 3:37).

Do you know Him? Then *hold fast the confidence and the **rejoicing** of the hope firm to the end* (Heb. 3:6).

Chapter Twenty

STAKE YOUR LIFE

...so will I go in unto the king, which is not according to the law: and if I perish I perish (Esther 4:16).

It takes warfare to actualize our blessings here on earth. The war is in the spiritual realm, not physical; it is a war of the mind, and it requires spiritual ammunition which God has made available to all His saints (Ps. 149:5-9). You must not only put on the whole armor of God: truth, righteousness, gospel of peace, faith, salvation, and word of God (Eph. 6:11, 14-17), but also consider yourself dead before you prayerfully engage in the war. In truth, you are a dead man, even though your bodymoves on the earth.

You died the day you received Jesus in your life, but your body did not drop dead because Jesus needs it to extend His work of grace to others (cf. Phil. 1:23-24). The life you have now is not yours but Christ's; therefore, your sufficiency is not in yourself but in Christ (2 Cor. 3:5). You are one with Him in the resurrection, ascension, and kingdom rule (Eph. 2:5-6): you are His *battle axe and weapons of war* (Jer. 51:20).

Paul testifies to this life of oneness with Christ: *I am crucified with Christ: nevertheless I live; yet not I, but Christ liveth in me: and the life which I now live in the flesh I live by the faith of the Son of God, who loved me, and gave himself for me* (Gal. 2:20).

You have nothing to fear for by faith you sit together with Jesus at God's right hand and operate from *the heavenly places far above all principality, and power, and might, and dominion, and every name that is named, not only in this world, but also in that which is to come* (Eph. 1:20-21; 2:6). You cannot go far in the Christian faith if you fear for yourlife here on earth. The devil will use the fear of death to intimidate and scare you any time you are making a strong advancement towards Jesus' warehouse to collect your consignments–blessings.

The trick here is that repeated warfare without spoils might cause burnout and over time, the individual quits trying and decides against the blessing, accepting to be a victim instead of a victor. But nothing, absolutely nothing, can stop you from advancing, if from the onset you concluded never to return except with your blessings, and you care little about dying.

Paul finished his course and ministry with joy because the gospel of Christ was more precious to him than his life (Acts 20:22-24; Phil. 1:20; cf. 2 Tim. 4:7-8). Queen Esther, who made the statement in our opening Scripture, did not die; rather, she became a channel of unprecedented deliverance, promotion, and blessings for her people [read the book of Esther to get the entire story yourself].

Our Lord Jesus no doubt redeemed us and restored our authority and inheritance on earth by His death (Rev. 5:12). *...for thou wast slain, and hast redeemed us to God by thy blood ... And hast made us unto our God kings and priests: and we shall **reign on earth*** (Rev. 5:9-10). But we will not realize and enjoy the inheritance if we do not use our authority on earth as kings and priests of God. God entrusts you with His authority: use it to the fullest without fear or apology to bring Him glory.

...be not afraid of them: remember the Lord, which is great and terrible, and fight for your brethren, your sons, and your daughters, your wives, and your houses (Neh. 4:14).

You must be both humble like a lamb and bold like a lion to get what belongs to you and others who God has placed in your custody. A lamb hurts no one, and no one frightens a lion. *...the righteous are as bold as a lion. A lion which is strongest among beasts, and turneth not away for any* (Prov. 28:1; 30:30).

> *Humility paves the way, boldness grabs it.*

Ignorance is at work if you are a Christian and still fear death. It means you are unaware of the victory you have over death and all evil through the blood of Jesus Christ (Heb. 2:14-15). Ignorance is a serious impediment to faith. You

> *Ignorance is disgusting, war against it.*

will not triumph over the devil, even though you are born again if you do battle against it by growing *in grace, and in the knowledge of our Lord and Saviour Jesus Christ* (2 Pet. 3:18; cf. 2 Tim.2:15).

And they overcame him [Satan] *by the blood of the Lamb, and by the word of their testimony; and they loved not their lives unto death* (Rev. 12:11).

A dead man is not afraid of death since he cannot die again. Defy the fear of death so that you can offer God the platform to display His power and glory through you, and possibly, many whom Satan entangles with diverse lusts and deceits will repent.

This life is only lived once and everyone must die eventually: take advantage of it. *What man is he that liveth, and shall not see death? Shall he deliver his soul from the hand of the grave* (Ps. 89:48)? You will not come back here again after you die (Job 7:9-10; 14:12). The devil deceives those who believe in reincarnation, and they waste their opportunities for repentance, assuming they will make amends when they return to this life again. *...it is appointed unto men once to die, but after this the judgment* (Heb. 9:27).

Death is a terror only to those who reject Christ or believers who serve themselves, and not to those who serve Christ (Heb. 2:14-16; Rom. 8:1; 2 Cor. 5:15). While sinners and disobedient children of God fear death, obedient children of God look towards it with fulfillment.

> *You are forever alive in Christ; death has no power over you.*

Death comes to committed believers not as a surprise, for God does not leave them in the dark about their earthly departure. He provides them with a clue about their death but not with a specific timeline so that they put their house in order (cf. Is. 38:1). Let us hear the words of four people who had an intimate relationship with God to confirm this: two each from the Old and New Testament.

1. Jacob to his sons: *And Israel said unto Joseph, Behold, **I die:** but God shall be with you, and bring you again unto the land of your fathers. And Jacob called unto his sons, and said, Gather*

yourselves together, that I may tell you that which shall befall you in the last days. And when Jacob had made an end of commanding his sons, he gathered up his feet into the bed, and yielded up the ghost, and was gathered unto his people (Gen. 48:21; 49:1, 33; cf. 50:24).

2. King David to his son, Solomon: *Now the days of David **drew near** that he should **die**, he charged his son, Solomon saying: I go the way of all the earth; be strong, therefore, and prove yourself a man* (1 Kin. 2:1-2).

3. Paul the apostle to his son in the Lord, Timothy: *I charge you… Preach the word! …fulfil your ministry. … the time of my departure is **at hand**. I have fought a good fight, I have finished the race, I have kept the faith. Finally, there is laid up for me the crown of righteousness…* (2 Tim. 4:1, 2, 5-8).

4. Peter the apostle to faithful brethren: *Yes, I think it is right, as long as I am in this tent, to stir you up by reminding you, knowing that **shortly** I must put off my tent, just as our Lord Jesus Christ showed me* (2 Pet. 1:13-14).

Life on earth is work. No one works all day without rest. But then, there is no true rest on earth. The place of true rest is in heaven. God our Father really delights in our homecoming after we have labored so we can rest. *Precious in the sight of the LORD is the death of his saints* (Ps. 116:15). Death is the transport that takes us out of this world and He will send it to bring us home at the appointed time. In the meantime, let us do our work, regardless.

Go therefore and make disciples all nations, baptizing them in the name of the Father and of the Son and of the Holy Spirit, teaching them to observe all things that I have commanded you; and, lo, I am with you always, even to the end of the age. Amen (Matt. 28:19-20).

For this God is our God for ever and ever: he will be our guide even unto death (Ps. 48:14).

Your time is in the hands of God and you will not die before your time if you walk in wisdom, *but live, and declare the works of the LORD* (Ps.

118:17; cf. 31:15). Death cannot work against us but for us as nothing works *against the truth but for the truth* (2 Cor. 13:8). *And we know that all things work together for good to those who love God, to those who are called according to His purpose* (Rom. 8:28).

Chapter Twenty-One

THE SOURCE

Then said Jesus to them again ... as my Father hath sent me, even so send I you (John 20:21).

We have discussed to a great length some behaviors that enable the Christian to live a triumphant life every day. Let us have an overview of their headings to refresh our memory; *faith, forgiveness, avoid foolishness, boldness, praises, disarmed by love, wisdom, no idols, self-defenseless, patience, being prayerful, no apology, keeping right companions, holding you responsible, operating from the victory point, be a giver, silence, hope against hope, rejoicing always, and stake your life.*

These behaviors are interconnected and none works successfully in isolation. We must be quick to add that no amount of self-effort, self-discipline, or human wisdom can make any person - even a Christian - bear the character. We bring it forth in complete and unflinching loyalty to the Holy Spirit.

But the fruit of the Spirit is love, joy, peace, longsuffering, gentleness, goodness, faith, meekness, temperance: against such there is no law. And they that are Christ's have crucified the flesh with the affections and lusts (Gal. 5:22-24).

The Holy Spirit bears other names, such as the Spirit of God, the Spirit of Christ, and the Spirit of grace (Rom. 8:9; Heb. 10:29). He reveals and enables believers to do the will of God (1 Cor. 2:10; Ezek. 36:27; cf. Zech. 12:10). He directs them on the path of truth and righteousness and provides them with power for service and exploits (John 16:13; Acts 1:8). Jesus could do nothing without the Holy Spirit: His conception, death, resurrection, ascension and everything He did on earth were by Him (Is. 11:1-4; Luke 1:34-35). He went into public ministry after the Father had baptized Him with the Holy Spirit.

*And Jesus, when he was baptized, went up straightway out of the water: and, lo, the heavens were opened unto him, and he saw the **Spirit of God** descending like a dove, and lighting upon him: And lo a voice from heaven, saying, This is my beloved Son, in whom I am well pleased* (Matt. 3:16-17). *How God anointed Jesus of Nazareth with the **Holy Spirit** and with **power**, who went about doing good, and healing all who were oppressed by the devil, for God was with him* (Acts 10:38).

Jesus denied Himself to do the will of His Father (Mark 14:36; cf. Phil. 2:5-8). He submitted Himself to the Spirit of God and became an instrument in His hand. He went about demonstrating the goodness of God by the power of the Holy Spirit. All the things Jesus did were the Father's design, and He did them by the guidance of God's Spirit.

*Then answered Jesus and said unto them, verily, verily, I say unto you, The Son can do nothing of himself, but what he seeth the Father do: for what things soever he doeth, these also doeth the Son likewise. I can of mine own self do nothing: as I hear, I judge: and my judgment is just; because **I seek not mine own will**, but will of the Father which hath sent me* (John 5:19, 30).

A leader goes in the direction he wants people to follow. Jesus lived an exemplary life of self-sacrifice. He showed His disciples that humility is the way to exaltation and that humiliation is part of the process (Heb. 12:2). He never asked them to do what He did not do. Neither did He ask them to do anything by their initiative nor strength for He too did nothing of Himself or by Himself. *For thou art the glory of their strength: and in thy favour our horn shall be exalted* (Ps. 89:17).

Jesus, shortly before His ascension, said to His disciples, *as my Father hath sent me, even so send I you* (John 20:21). The Father sent Him out for service with the power of the Holy Spirit after His baptism (Matt. 3:16-17; Luke 4:1, 14-15). Jesus had to empower His disciples with that same Holy Spirit so that their lives and service would evidence His life and work as well, but He would first get back to heaven for His Spirit to take over them (John 16:7).

On the last day, that great day of the feast, Jesus stood and cried out, saying, If anyone thirsts, let him come to Me and drink. He who believes *in Me, as the Scripture has said, **out of his heart will flow rivers of living water**. But this He spoke concerning **the Spirit**, whom those believing in Him would receive; for the Holy Spirit was **not yet** given; because Jesus was **not yet glorified**.* (John 7:37-39).

The power of the Holy Spirit is all that the disciples need for efficacy. Therefore, Jesus instructed them to remain in Jerusalem until He baptizes them with the Holy Spirit.

*And being assembled together with them, He commanded them not to depart from Jerusalem, but wait for the promise of the Father… But you shall receive **power** when the **Holy Spirit** has come **upon** you; and you shall be **witnesses** to Me in Jerusalem, and in all Judaea and Samaria, and to the end of the earth* (Acts 1:4, 8).

The disciples remained in Jerusalem praying in harmony, and afterward the Holy Spirit came upon them. The evidence was not only the foreign languages by which they declared the awesome works of God but also their exposure to ridicule and troubles (Acts 2:11-13; cf. Acts 10:44-46; 19:6; 4:1-3; cf. Luke 4:1ff). Note that each believer spoke in tongues as directed by the Holy Spirit; the languages were not artificial, and neither did they learn them. Tongues are a sign to unbelievers and not to believers (1 Cor. 14:22a).

*And when the day of Pentecost had fully come… Then there appeared to them divided tongues, as of fire, and one sat upon each of them. And they were all filled with the Holy Spirit and began to **speak with other tongues**, as the Spirit gave them utterance* (Acts 2:1, 3-4).

God's love for humanity is incomprehensible; He provided them an opportunity in Christ to escape His impending judgment for sin, which originated with Adam in the Garden of Eden (Gen. 2:15-17; 3:6-7, 23-24). His promise to pour out His Spirit to humankind before the great judgment became a reality on the day of Pentecost because of the finished work of grace at the Calvary by the resurrected and exalted Jesus (Joel 2:28-31). On that day, His Spirit indwelt the disciples: the church of Christ, to continue His work through them.

While Peter addressed the crowd who took them for alcoholics, he clearly explained that the gift of the Holy Spirit was by the benevolence of Jesus. God bequeathed all He has to His beloved Son, Jesus, through whom alone He fulfills all His promises to man and will execute His judgment on man (John 3:35; 16:15; Acts 17:31). *For it pleased the Father that in him should all fullness dwell* (Col. 1:19).

*...Jesus of Nazareth, a Man attested by God to you by miracles, wonders, and signs which **God did through Him** in your mist ... Therefore being exalted to the right hand of God, and **having received from the Father** the promise of the Holy Spirit, He poured out this, which you now see and hear* (Acts 2:22, 33).

Jesus Christ is the Source of the Christian character, for by His shed blood God grants man salvation and gives him the Holy Spirit. He alone baptizes with the Holy Spirit and with fire, as John, His forerunner, openly states:

I indeed baptize you with water unto repentance, but He who is coming after me is mightier than I, whose sandals I am not worthy to carry. He will baptize you with the Holy Spirit and fire (Matt. 3:11; cf. Acts 1:4-5).

The indwelling presence of the Holy Spirit in the life of a believer is the inhabiting of both the Son and the Father in the believer (John 14:23; Eph. 2:22). The God who walked the earth through Jesus is in His disciples and is operating through them by the power of His Spirit. You **cannot** have the Holy Spirit **without accepting Jesus Christ as your Savior.**

Chapter Twenty-Two

POWER: THE INDISPENSABLE NEED OF THE CHRISTIAN

And be not drunk with wine; but be filled with the Spirit (Eph. 5:18).

After Jesus baptized His disciples with the Holy Spirit and they spoke in tongues, the unbelieving crowd assumed they were drunks (Acts 2:13). Being a drunkard is not a virtue but a vice. However, the attitudes of drunkards can provoke us to a life of devotion to God if we objectively consider them.

Our opening Scripture is the statement of the apostle Paul to Christians in Ephesus. For him to say to the believers, *be not drunk with wine; but be filled with the Spirit,* shows that there is a correlation between the influence of wine and the impact of the Holy Spirit. *Give strong drink unto him that is ready to perish, and wine unto those that be of heavy heart. Let him drink and forget his poverty, and remember his misery no more* (Prov. 31:6-7).

The above Scriptures clarify that before someone becomes alcohol dependent, he must have seen his condition as insurmountable and accepted helplessness and hopelessness. Alcohol dulls the drinker's memory and allows him to live in euphoria while denying his problems. The drunk is carefree. Whether or not his problems increase, he seeks more wine because of the wild feelings he derives from intoxication.

Who hath woe? who hath sorrow? who hath contentions? who hath babbling? who hath wounds without cause? who hath redness of eyes? They that tarry long at the wine; they that go to seek mixed wine. Look not upon wine when it is red, when it giveth his colour in the cup, when it moveth itself aright. At last it biteth like a serpent, and stingeth like an adder. Thine eyes shall behold strange women, and thine heart shall utter perverse things. Yea, thou shalt be as he that lieth down in the midst of the sea, or as he that lieth upon the top of a mast. They have stricken me, shalt thou say, and I was not sick; they have beaten me, and I felt it not: **when shall I awake? I will seek it again** (Prov. 23:29-35).

> **Wine stirs up and overpowers the drunk.**

From this Scripture, we can observe that the drunk enthusiastically expresses his lustful desires and glories in his shame. He boldly and freely says or does things that ordinarily he would not say or do. Intoxication removes all his inhibitions and his wild actions delude him into thinking he has found peace and joy. Peace and joy make the heart healthy and stable; only the Holy Spirit can supply them. But wine provides a cheap alternative and is a dangerous trap for multitudes who resort to it, seeking a solution.

As the drunk gave up and surrendered to wine, so must the believer (*who desires to be filled with the Holy Spirit*) totally deny himself. He must come to the end of himself and submit to the Holy Spirit for empowerment. Both a drunkard and a Spirit-filled believer will do incredible things, but their deeds would differ just like their sources do.

The drunk is strong in evil and acts compulsively to the delight of the devil. The Spirit-filled believer is bold in the righteousness of Christ, but is conscious and conscientious of his acts. The Holy Spirit neither imposes Himself on him nor overrules his will; he is at liberty to obey or reject His guidance. Although the Holy Spirit provides a believer with supernatural abilities to overcome his corrupt human nature, the application of such abilities depends solely on the believer's choice (Rom. 7:22-23; Gal. 5:16-17; cf. Eph. 5:18-21).

*...***work out** *your own salvation with fear and trembling. For it is God which* **worketh in** *you both to will and to do of his good pleasure* (Phil. 2:12b-13).

Miracles are the daily bread of a believer who lives according to the revelations and guidance of the Holy Spirit; signs and wonders characterize his life. Walking in the power of the Holy Spirit is the right of every believer, but only those who walk in obedience to faith experience it.

The outpouring of the Holy Spirit, which began with the first generation of believers in Christ on the day of Pentecost, remains valid and vital until the second coming of Jesus. It is for every believer: the young and old, male and female, the educated and uneducated, the rich and the poor, parents and children, the Jews and the Gentiles (Acts 2:39; cf. Joel 2:28-29; 9:17; 10:34-35, 44; 11:17-18; 19:1-6; Acts).

Jesus' command for His disciples to stay in Jerusalem until they become baptized with the Holy Spirit was insightful and instructive (Acts 1:4). After the resurrection, Jesus breathed on His disciples and they received the Holy Spirit (John 20:22), yet they had to wait for the promise of the Father. The breath of Jesus to His disciples, which gave them life in the Spirit, is comparable to the breath of God that gave life to the soul of man at creation (Gen. 2:7). As the breath of God distinguished man from animals and other creatures and placed him above them (Ps. 8:6; cf. Gen. 1:27-28), so the breath of Christ differentiates a believer from the pagan and gives him the power of sonship (John 1:12; Rom. 8:16).

A believer's first duty is not to engage in public ministry after his conversion, but to get into a private deeper relationship with the Holy Spirit by whom he differs from the world and has the right of inheritance (cf. Gal. 1:10-12, 15-17). Jesus knew the dangers that awaited His disciples in their assignments and would not send them to the field as amateurs and unarmed, hence the command to wait. He too waited for the Father's empowerment before His outdoor ministry (John 7:2-4; 6, 8; cf. Luke 4:1, 14).

Wait for God's power before public engagement.

We cannot stand against the onslaught of evil spirits and the world's system without being dead to self and unite with the Holy Spirit (John 14:20; cf. Acts 15:28; Ezra 7:18). Simon Peter, who by self-confidence genuinely insisted he would not deny Jesus for whatever reason, did so blatantly when housemaids accosted him. But this same Peter who was timid before house-helps and denied Jesus; and other disciples who distanced themselves from Jesus during crucifixion and thereafter hid for fear of the Jews, withstood the mammoth crowd and challenges the *'who is who'* of the temple after the Holy Spirit baptism (Matt. 26:31, 33-35, 58, 69-75; Mark 14:50; Luke 23:49; John 20:19a; cf. Acts 2:5-6; 4:19-20; 5:29).

The disciples' devotion to God after the baptism was unparalleled; they sold themselves to Christ. The baptism of fire burned every limiting character in them and purified their hearts. The love of God consumed them and they became one with God on purpose. Nothing mattered to them anymore but the salvation of men, which is the primary concern of God. They had the right perspective regarding spiritual works and directed their war against evil spirits instead of their fellow human beings who were in captivity of the devil and needed salvation. In their war for the souls of men, they endured afflictions even death, knowing that in Christ they live whether alive or dead (Rom. 14:8; Phil. 1:21; cf. John 3:16).

While they untiringly rescued the souls of men from destruction, they maintained a life of holiness, refusing to soil their garments and become unfit for heaven at the end of their service on earth (Is. 35:8; Heb. 12:14; Jude 21-23). Their commitment proved that the Holy Spirit baptism exposes self and transforms the believer, and that the grace of God works effectively when self is out of the way.

The coldness and levity with which many Christians today relate to God and handle His work reveals the missing ministry of the Holy Spirit in their lives. Each believer must by themselves earnestly desire and pray for the baptism of the Holy Spirit after conversion to enable them function effectively in their various individual offices, including marriage, which is the number one and most crucial ministry of every believing husband and wife. The Holy Spirit will certainly rest on any disciple who prayerfully waits in expectation like the first time disciples of Christ. *Blessed are they which do hunger and thirst after righteousness: for they shall be filled* (Matt. 5:6).

The Holy Spirit identifies a sinner as a child of God when He comes **into** him at conversion and endows him with power for service when He comes **upon** him at baptism. Paul's question to the disciples he met at Ephesus and his subsequent actions is proof that the Holy Spirit must empower a believer after regeneration for functionality.

...And finding some disciples he said unto them, Did you receive the Holy Spirit when you believed? When they heard this, they were baptized in the name of the Lord Jesus. And when Paul had laid hands on them, the Holy Spirit came **upon** *them, and they* **spoke with tongues** *and* **prophesied** (Acts 19:1-2, 5-6).

Again, Peter and John had to pray for the Samaritan believers to be baptized in the Holy Spirit after they received salvation during Philip's evangelistic work.

Now when the apostles who were at Jerusalem heard that Samaria had received the word of God, they sent Peter and John to them, who, when they were come down, prayed for them that they might receive the Holy Spirit. For as yet He had fallen <u>upon</u> none of them. They had only been <u>baptized in the name</u> of the Lord Jesus. Then they laid hands on them, and they received the Holy Spirit (Acts 8:14-17).

While on the way to a murder mission, Saul of Tarsus [Paul the Apostle] embraced Jesus as his Savior and Lord, but he underwent baptism with the Holy Spirit before he began spreading the gospel of Christ (Acts 9:4-6, 17-18, 20). God, who confirms our sonship by His Spirit indwelling us, also empowers us for service with that same Spirit if we are obedient (Rom. 8:11; Acts 5:32).

All the people who proved the power of God in their services both in the Old and New Testament did so by God's Spirit (Micah 3:8; Acts 1:8). They accomplished nothing by human intelligence or efforts, but by the power of the Spirit. The Holy Spirit provided opportunities, guidance, and power as they made themselves available (John 16:12-13; cf. 14:26).

> **We succeed by the power of the Holy Spirit.**

The power of God, which causes genuine signs, wonders and miracles, is at work when we work with His Spirit (Luke 5:17; Heb. 2:3-4). *...Not by might, nor by power, but by my spirit, saith the LORD of hosts* (Zech.

4:6b). *So then it is not of him that willeth, nor of him that runneth, but of God that sheweth mercy* (Rom. 9:16).

The Holy Spirit is the Spirit of grace, and He enables us to do the will of God despite temptations for *where sin abounded, grace did much more abound* (Rom. 5:20). We stress and weary ourselves and live like beggars when we take the grace of God in vain or linger over what God asks us to do (cf. 2 Cor. 6:1). Disobedience hinders the Holy Spirit and hurts us (Jer. 25:7).

A life of total allegiance to the Holy Spirit is possible only when we deny self: give up our own will and accept God's will in every situation. The purifying work of the Holy Spirit makes sin infertile in the hearts of obedient believers (1 John 3:3, 9) and also nullifies class distinction (Acts 15:8-9; Gal. 3:28; 1 Cor. 12:13).

A believer who lives for self satisfies corrupt human nature, which is obsessed with lustful desires and seeks earthly glory. Every disciple of Christ in any generation who desires to manifest the life and power of Christ must reject lustful desires and spurn the glory of this world as Jesus did (Luke 4:5-8). *...Whoever desires to come after Me, let him deny himself, and take up his cross, and follow Me* (Mark 8:34).

Self-sacrifice is a prerequisite for discipleship and satisfactory service (Rom. 12:1). We will overcome a life of disobedience that strengthens self, if our love for God is without reservation like that of our Lord Jesus and faithful brethren who face various trials, even horrifying death, rather than gratify self (Mark 14:36; John 14:30-31; 19:17-18a; Dan. 6:5, 8, 10, 16a; Acts 12:1-4; cf. John 14:15).

Truly, Satan opposes every initiative or move of the Holy Spirit in our lives, but he will definitely fail if he cannot find sin in us (Dan. 6:4, 22; John 14:30). *All unrighteousness is sin* (1 John 5:17a).

Sin is opposition to God. It is Satan's property that gives him the right to brutalize anyone in possession it. Any Christian who toys with sin and wars against the hosts of darkness becomes a casualty of sin. You

> **Sin makes someone worthless.**

cannot dictate to the devil when you are playing his games, and are a prisoner in his camp. Sin saps spiritual energy and renders a Christian invalid. *For my life is spent with grief, and my years with sighing: my strength faileth because of mine iniquity, and my bones are consumed* (Ps. 31:10).

The actuality of the Christian freedom and authority lies in a life of holiness. Therefore, a Christian must prioritize the instructions and directions of the Holy Spirit and duly obey them in order to mature and walk in power.

But the anointing which ye have received of him abideth in you, and ye need not that any man teach you: but as the same anointing teacheth you of all things, and is truth, and is no lie, and even as it hath taught you, ye shall abide in him (1 John 2:27).

Obedience to God strengthens your spirit and makes you confident: you increasingly realize who you are in Christ and exercise your authority more boldly. A Christian is obedient to the Holy Spirit as long as he remembers that *the kingdom of God is not eating and drinking; but righteousness and peace and joy in the Holy Spirit* (Rom. 14:17; cf. Heb. 13:9). If he forgets this truth, he will spurn the counsel of the Spirit and walk after his own sinful human nature to the detriment of his eternal salvation (Rom. 8:1).

God's intention is not for us to drop out of salvation, but we have to make a choice between the leadership of the Holy Spirit and the self (Rom. 8:1, 14; cf. Matt. 16:24-25). We cannot surrender to both self and the Holy Spirit at the same time; one must give way for the other (Gal. 5:16-17).

Self leads to ultimate failure, but the Spirit gives power for victory (Prov. 14:12; John 6:63). A Christian who lives for self, that is occupied with his own ambition instead of Christ's, is practically no different from an unbeliever and will fall when faced with persecution (Matt. 13:20-22). Persecution - righteous suffering - is a lifelong blessed inheritance of all Christians who walk after the righteousness of Christ (2 Tim. 3:12; 1 Thess. 3:3-4).

The knowledge of Christ includes sharing both in His resurrection power and sufferings (Phil. 1:29; 3:10). The Christian behaviors we have discussed are, therefore, not sporadic conduct in a 'good mood' moment, but the lifestyle of the Christian who walks with the Holy Spirit in his various relationships and businesses.

Someone can receive salvation and the Holy Spirit baptism simultaneously, as the case of the Gentiles in the book of Acts (Chapter 10:44-48) or after some time ((Acts 8:14-17). The crux of the matter is that the Holy Spirit baptism is a separate and definite experience after regeneration, regardless of whether someone receives it at a new birth or after a while.

It is a onetime experience that empowers the believer for service. God did not baptize Jesus twice with the Holy Spirit, and neither did Jesus baptize the disciples twice. The believer who receives baptism with the Holy Spirit does not need to be baptized repeatedly, but must constantly seek to be filled with the Spirit. Do you buy a new phone any time your battery runs down or charge it? Do you replace your generator with a new one when it runs out of fuel or refill its tank?

A disciple who manifests the power of the Holy Spirit spends virtue (cf. Mark 5:30; Luke 6:19) and needs a steady supply of power from the Holy Spirit for sustenance and greater efficiency. Such a disciple receives the anointing through fellowshipping with the Holy Spirit in prayer and studying the Word. The anointing will elude him if he does not humble himself before God (James 4:10). Then he will vacillate, faint in well doing, fall, and may walk in ultimate discouragement and return to the world despite the gentle nudges and encouragements of the Holy Spirit.

The early disciples continually seek God's presence for greater anointing to preach the gospel of Christ despite that the same preaching exposed them to various sufferings like battering, imprisonments, threats, and death.

And being let go, they went to their own companions and reported all that the chief priests and elders had said to them. And when they **had prayed***, the place where they were assembled together was shaken; and they were* **all filled with the Holy Spirit***, and they spoke the word of God with* **boldness** *(Acts 4:23, 31; cf. Acts 4:3, 18; 5:18, 40; cf. 7:59).*

In summary, the individual members of the church or the entire church can accomplish nothing without the power of the Holy Spirit, and that power comes as they become loyal to Christ, for *the Lord is that Spirit* (1 Cor. 3:17; cf. John 14:17-18; John 15:5). The productivity of each believer depends on their intimacy with God's Spirit, who supplies power to His saints.

The early disciples mirrored Christ in character and in demonstration of power because they were under His Lordship and served by the power of His Spirit for His glory. They wholeheartedly relied on the Holy Spirit for everything (Acts 15:28; 16:6-7). The church of Christ in any generation cannot behave differently if they are to exercise the authority of Christ and experience His victory in their lives and ministries.

Chapter Twenty-Three

DOING: EXPERIENCE AND BLESSING

...Ezra had prepared his heart to seek the Law of the LORD, and to <u>do</u> it, and to teach statutes and ordinances in Israel (Ezra 7:10).

And He says to him, "You have answered rightly; <u>do</u> this and you will live." And he says, "He who showed mercy on him." Then Jesus said to him, "Go and <u>do</u> likewise." (Luke 10:28, 37).

If ye know these things, happy are ye if ye <u>do</u> them (John 13:17).

In the above Scriptures, we underlined the word 'do' to draw attention to the primary message of this chapter. The key emphasis of the four verses is Application - doing results in practical knowledge and good understanding (John 7:17; Ps.111:10b). There is no way we can confirm if the promises of God are true or not unless we do what the Scripture say (John 7:17). If one cannot prove what he claims to know, it means he has only the head knowledge of it and not the experiential knowledge.

Christianity is not just in words but in doing too; it is not theoretical but practical. It is not in giving the right answers about issues, but also in the right application of the answers to the issues. Christianity is not about forming organizations or addressing people *with enticing words of man's wisdom*, but walking with the Holy Spirit and manifesting the power of God (1 Cor. 2:4).

Transfer of knowledge is effective when the life of a teacher reflects his message. No one can prove the kingdom of God by observation, but by a transformed life. The personality of the one who proclaims the word of God should mirror the biblical truth, he declares. Otherwise, he uses the Word as a tool for mind control and attack (Micah 3:5).

Theoretical or rhetorical theologians are charlatans who add to the confusion and problems of people as they lack the experience of salvation. They misrepresent the love of Christ, promote vanity, and perpetuate slavery. They hypnotize their hearers with charming words and these poor fellows, despite the contradiction between their commitment and expectations (especially lack of peace and freedom from sin) cannot stop and ask, 'Is the Spirit of God behind these words? Does God not deliver people from bondage? Do God's blessings add sorrow? (cf. Micah 2:7, Prov. 10:22).

A person cannot work in opposition to God's principles and raise Christians who walk in the truth. Your conduct, more than your words, shows who you are. Jesus Christ, who is our High Priest and Model and Mentor, began both to <u>do</u> and teach, proving He lived the life He taught (Acts 1:1). You will understand Scriptures better when you do them, then you will talk less and pray more for the kingdom of God is not in word, but in power (1 Cor. 4:20).

Christianity is following the footsteps of Christ in living to please God and persuading or encouraging others to do the same. It is spreading the love of God to people by the power of His Spirit. A Christian should neither condemn sinners nor condone sin; but preach the gospel of Christ to sinners, appealing for their repentance so they can receive forgiveness from God and have a new life in Christ.

A preacher who condemns sinners instead of sin is guilty of assuming the prerogative of God and ignorantly closing the door of mercy against himself (cf. James 4:11-12; Rom. 14:4a; Luke 6:37). Jesus Himself stated clearly that He did not come to search for people's sin but to deliver them from it. *For the Son man is not come to destroy men's life, but to save them* (Luke 9:56). *For God sent not his Son into the world to condemn the world; but that the world through him might be saved* (John 3:17).

> **True Christian loves sinners but condemns their unrighteous acts.**

However, a preacher who condones sin and assures his hearers of many blessings from God (including eternal life in heaven), lives in deceit and propagates falsehood to his own destruction (2 Tim. 3:13; Phil. 3:18-19;

cf. Jude 11-12). His approval of someone making heaven without holiness is like assuring a lazy student that he will win a school scholarship award designated for the best student of the year (Heb. 12:14; cf. John 8:31-32). There is no shortcut to heaven; holiness remains the way in every generation (Heb. 12:14; cf. Is. 35:8).

Eternal salvation is the greatest of all blessings, and Christians who hope for heaven must pay primary attention to their spiritual needs. Material blessings are a part of the salvation package and they overtake a believer while he pursues the kingdom of God in righteousness (Matt. 6:32-33; Deut. 28:1-2).

Righteousness results in persecution but bears immeasurable rewards. A believer may lose precious relationships, privileges, or things and suffer for his insistence on God's standards, but eventually recover them in a greater dimension besides eternal life. A life of righteousness attracts and preserves blessings and nullifies the desires of the wicked (cf. Ps. 112).

Wealth and riches are ours in Christ; we inherit them in righteousness. Our Lord Jesus, in answering Peter's question about the benefits of rendering unreserved service to Him, revealed that He honors anyone who devotes himself to Him and His course with both material and spiritual success.

Then answered Peter and said unto him, Behold, we have forsaken all, and followed thee; what shall we have therefore (Matt. 19:27)?

*And Jesus answered and said, Verily I say unto you, there is **no man** that hath **left** house, or brethren, or sisters, or father, or mother, or wife, or children, or lands for **my sake, and the gospel's**. But he shall **receive a hundredfold now in this time**, houses, and brethren, and sisters, and mothers, and children, and lands, **with persecutions**; and in the **world to come eternal life** (Mark 10:29-30).*

Jesus' statement, apart from confirming that the Christian prosperity and righteous suffering—persecution—goes hand in hand, also shows that it is holistic. It covers every aspect of the believer's life: his business, family, and life after death [Jesus' omission of wife in the abundance of things to receive is not an error but proof that marriage between one man and one woman until death separates them is the standard of God

(1 Cor. 7:11, 39; cf. Matt. 19:3-6)]. This is indeed a balance prosperity in which the Scripture and the Holy Spirit rule your spirit, soul, and body for unity of purpose (cf. Deut. 11:18; Ps 119:9-11). The agreement among the 'three' you enables you to work in agreement with God and experience His faithfulness in every aspect of you while you rest in His care and love.

The essence of salvation is to save man from the wrath of God that will consume all His enemies who delight in evil and spurn or abuse the grace He offered all humanity through the sacrificial death of His Only Son, Jesus, for them to live a righteous and holy life; a life that glorifies Him (1 Thess. 5:9; Rev. 7:9, 13-14; cf. 6:15-17; 20:15; Heb. 10:26-29).

Every believer can escape eternal punishment in the lake of fire, but earthly glory can easily lure those who prioritize their physical needs over their spiritual needs and, as a result, they disregard the righteousness of God in their dealings. Many so-called believers find it hard to practice righteousness because they see only the suffering that comes with it and not the rewards attached. Those who will survive righteous suffering must look beyond mockery, scourging, and crucifixion to see the resurrection: the glory ahead (Matt. 20:19).

Suffering, though not pleasant in whatever way, can **make** you if you interpret your experiences positively and take advantage of them to learn obedience to God (Heb. 5:8; cf. 12:11). But it can **mar** you if you have a negative perspective and bear grudges. The former makes you a victor, while the latter makes you either an oppressor or a victim.

Someone can be a Christian and still be an oppressor or a victim: it is a matter of choosing to either submit self to the Holy Spirit and *die daily* to the lust of the corrupt human nature or to surrender to self and satisfy the sinful desires (1 Cor. 15:31b; Gal. 5:16-17, 24; Col. 3:5; Rom. 8:36).

An oppressor can be materially successful and momentarily happy, but can never have peace or joy. Happiness is circumstantial and superficial; it comes from good happenings of the moments. *Even in laughter the heart is sorrowful; and the end of that mirth is heaviness* (Prov. 14:13).

Peace and joy always go together and are inherent in salvation; we enjoy them even at the most difficult times, because they result from spiritual well-being (2 Cor. 6:10). When peace is absent, do not bother looking for joy. *For ye shall go out with joy, and be led forth with peace...* (Is. 55:12).

> *Every other blessing is available for man without faith in Christ except eternal peace and joy.*

A victim may not be spiritually or materially established. His feelings fluctuate, and he is mostly gloomy. A victor has holistic prosperity (3 John 2). He lives beyond happiness; his dominant emotions are peace and joy. However, his satisfaction is not from obedience to works, but the grace, available only in Christ (Eph. 2:8-9).

Man, in his best ability, is still man and can accomplish nothing noteworthy before God without the grace of God working in his life. *But by the grace of God I am what I am: and his grace which was bestowed upon me was not in vain; but I laboured more abundantly than they all:* ***yet not I, but the grace of God which was with me*** (1 Cor. 15:10).

You do not become a champion in any game without first learning the rules of the game and then practicing them correctly. Likewise, you do not become materially successful because you choose to be an oppressor, or have holistic [balanced] prosperity because you decide to be a victor. You have to first learn the principles and use them judiciously in whichever class you belong to; otherwise, you remain a victim. A victim delights only in mere talk, which inclines to *penury* (Prov. 14:23). He lacks the wisdom and power to translate his ideas into profitable deeds.

An oppressor uses Satan's ideology (the world's wisdom) to transact business. He intimidates and cheats people, but most often in disguise. He feeds on the victim but dreads the victor. A victor operates in the power of the Holy Spirit (Luke 10:18-19, Act 1:8), and stands on the victory of Christ and accepts nothing less. He, in compassion, helps others to develop their gifts and businesses. A victim accommodates his problems and seeks people's sympathy rather than face and overcome them.

The oppressor lives for himself and the victim for the oppressor, but both of them ignorantly and indirectly promote the kingdom of darkness through ungodly lifestyles (Gal. 5:19-21). They depend on themselves and frustrate the grace of God (cf. Gal. 2:21). Hence, they are stuck in the kindergarten class of Christianity, remaining toys in the hands of evil spirits (1 Cor. 3:1, 3).

> *Only babies feel comfortable in playgroup.*

To be a Christian is not to be an oppressor. To be a Christian is not to be a victim. To be a Christian is to be a victor–it is to have unbroken fellowship with the resurrected Christ through His Spirit and show forth His glory in every aspect of our life (Acts 11:26). A Christian believes in the death, burial, and resurrection of Jesus Christ (1 Cor. 15:1, 3), and lives by the power of the resurrection, which puts him far above all powers of darkness.

> *A Christian reflects the heart and character of Christ.*

Each believer has to choose from these three identity options: oppressor, victim, and victor. No one can dodge it; you must be one.

We conclude that all the things discussed so far will benefit us only when we put them into practice daily. Just as you cannot know the taste of a meal by its smell, you also cannot know the effect of knowledge by merely reading or hearing it. Doing the will of God is proof we belong to His family. *For whosoever shall do the will of God, the same is my brother, and my sister, and mother* (Mark 3:35). You will accomplish whatever God commissioned you to do when you apply biblical truth and rely on the Holy Spirit.

Chapter Twenty-Four

THE TRUE SPIRITUALITY

Does the eagle mount up at your command, and make her nest on high?
She dwelleth and abideth on the rock, upon the crag of the rock, and the
stronghold. From thence she seeketh the prey, and her eyes behold afar off
(Job 39:27-29).

The Christian who walks in the Spirit does things only as Jesus commands. He is like an eagle which builds its nest at high altitude for safety and visibility. Such a believer flies in the atmosphere of faith, stands on the promises of God, and is unmoved by the circumstances of life, knowing by experience that all things work for his good (Rom. 8:28).

He is intentional about his actions and conscious of his heavenly citizenship as he is in a deep relationship with the Holy Spirit, who reveals to him the mind of God on issues of life and guides his footsteps (1 Cor. 9:26-27; 2:10, 12).

He is discreet and wise and lives a sanctified life; a life devoted to God (Gen. 39:7-9; 41:39; Acts 4:19-20; 5:29; Gal. 1:10). He knows his God and is strong in the Lord, and does exploits for God's own purpose and glory among the deceived and the corrupt (Dan. 11:32).

By this lifestyle, the Spirit-filled believer is dead to self, grows in the grace and rooted in the knowledge of Christ and enjoys the freedom he has in Christ - freedom from sin, Satan, self, traditionalism, the obscene world system, penury, and ignorance. In fact, freedom from everything that limits the life of fullness Christ brought us.

The perfect will of God is that we live a balanced life, glorifying Him in every aspect of our life. As life is not about satisfying self but pleasing God, the sole focus of the spiritual believer is to discover the mind of God on all occasions and do His will. His prosperity lies in doing God's will, not his.

*I have come that they may have life, and that they may have it **more abundantly**. Until now you have asked nothing in My name. Ask, and you will receive, that your **joy may be full**. And of his **fulness** have all we **received**, and grace for grace. Grace and truth came by Jesus Christ* (John 10:10b; 16:24; 1:16,17b).

A spiritual believer suffers only what God, in His wisdom, permits in order to further his maturity. He admits his weaknesses and accepts God's grace to sail through life's test. *For this thing I besought the Lord thrice, that it might depart from me. And he said unto me, My grace is sufficient for thee: for my strength is made perfect in weakness. Most gladly therefore will I rather glory in my infirmities, that the power of Christ may rest upon me* (2 Cor. 12:8-9).

Such a believer operates in the Spirit and gives no room for the gratification of sinful desires. His deep concern is to live in the fullness of Christ (Eph. 3:19; Col. 1:19; John 1:16) and prove His victory in all aspects of life. He lives for Christ and his major goal is to win souls for Him (Prov. 14:25a). He is indeed a victor in Christ by the strength of God. Jesus saved us to live for Him and accomplish His purpose; He did not save us simply to live for ourselves, other people, or for societal approval.

And that he [Jesus] *died for all, that they which live should not henceforth live unto themselves, but unto him which died for them, and rose again* (2 Cor. 5:15).

The spiritual believer, as a true ambassador of Christ, brings heaven's blessings down to earth and takes the glory back to heaven. Living and making daily profits for our Lord Jesus is a great pleasure. Satan hates it and works assiduously to make us overlook the abundant benefits of salvation or pursue them to the detriment of our souls. The earth and everything in it is our Father's estate and property; we inherit it by trusting in the finished works of Christ and enjoy them in the presence of God (Ps. 24:1-2; Is. 54:14; Rev. 5:9-10, 12).

> *You serve humanity through Jesus Christ.*

For anyone to strike a balance in his Christian life and everyday routines, his heart must always rest in God while his hands are on activities.

That means he cannot separate his Christian faith from his daily duties, whether at home, in the school, workplace, or anywhere else. His works must show his faith. Such a person does *not trust in uncertain riches, but in the living God, who giveth us richly all things to enjoy* (1 Tim. 6:17)!

Chapter Twenty-Five

THE BENEFITS OF TRUSTING GOD

Oh how great is thy goodness, which thou hast laid up for them that fear thee; which thou hast wrought for them that trust in thee before the sons of men (Ps. 31:19).

As you trust God, you watch Him cover your sins and turn your curses to blessings (Is. 1:18; Ps. 32:1; cf. Gal. 3:13-14), your fear to faith, your ignorance to knowledge, your depression to hope, your hardships to tenacity, your troubles to testimonies, your desertions to devotion (2 Tim. 1:15; 4:10a, 16-17; cf. Ps. 27:10; Is. 49:15), your deformation to transformation, your calamities to creativity, your pain to praise, your confusion to concentration, your scandal to sanctification, your lousiness to holiness, your cry to laughter, your delay to discovery, your commotion to peace, your denial to acceptance, your rejection to recognition, yourshame to glory (Zeph. 3:19).

He will turn your humiliation to exaltation, your dungeon to palace, your hate to eternal excellency (Is. 60:15), your mistakes to wisdom, your disappointments to faithfulness, your dishonor to honor, your disgrace to grace, your demotion to promotion, your weakness to strength, your criticism to character, your frustrations to progress, your unemployment to entrepreneurship, your barrenness to plenty (1 Sam. 2:5), your penury to charity, your mockery to manifestation, your scorners to advertisers (Ps. 126:1-2), your nightmares to wonders, your caricature to crowning, your struggle to victory, and your tears to joy.

You have turned for me my mourning into dancing; You have put off my sackcloth and clothed me with gladness, To the end that my glory may sing praise to You and not be silent. O LORD my God, I will give thanks to You forever (Ps. 30:11-12).

Whom God blesses, no one can curse and when He opens a door, no one can close it (Num. 23:8; Rev. 3:7). All the wickedness of men to you produces the goodness of God in you and to you when you wholeheartedly put your confidence in God and faithfully follow the leading of His Spirit. There is no loss in trusting and obeying God. Everything is gain.

*My brethren, count it all joy when ye fall into diverse temptations; Knowing this, that the trying of your faith worketh patience. But let patience have her perfect work, that ye may be **perfect** and **entire**, **wanting nothing*** (James 1:2-4).

Oh, taste and see that the LORD is good; Blessed is the man who trusts in Him! Oh, fear the LORD, you His saints! There is no want to those who fear Him. The young lions lack and suffer hunger; But those who seek the LORD shall not lack any good thing (Ps. 34:8-10).

AFTERWORDS

For all that is in the world, the lust of the flesh, and the lust of the eyes, and the pride of life, is not of the Father, but of the world. And the world passeth away, and the lust thereof: but he that doeth the will of God abideth for ever (1 John 2:16-17).

Dear friend, what a journey this has been!

I thank God for His grace that enabled you to go through this book and for the new life we have in Christ Jesus. Until you see God in heaven, do not at any point feel that you have arrived. It is obvious from our opening Scripture that earthly blessings and pleasures are transitory and nothing to compare with our reward in the world to come (Eph. 2:7). Therefore, they should not blind you from daily holy living. Our destination is heaven, not this world. I earnestly desire to see you at the Lord's marriage supper (Rev. 19:9).

Be resolute in your choice to live for Jesus Christ, our Lord, and let the joy of your awaiting crown of righteousness override other concerns. Material blessings are certain, and you will not fall for them if you have no attachment to things that lack eternal value. Your lifestyle on earth will determine your eternal destiny (2 Cor. 5:10).

Maintain a balanced prosperity. If you can't, it is better to be rich spiritually and wallow in material poverty like Lazarus and eventually make heaven than to be wealthy but a pauper spiritually, and at your death demons receive your soul to spend eternity with them in flames like the arrogant rich man (Luke 16:19-24; cf. Matt. 25:34). May none of us be among those that shall receive this pronouncement from the Judge of the whole earth: *...Depart from me, ye cursed, into everlasting fire, prepared for the devil and his angels* (Matt. 25:41).

Consider these parting words of Brother Paul to Brother Timothy and remain focused.

You therefore must endure hardship as a good soldier of Jesus Christ. No one engaged in warfare entangles himself with the affairs of this life, that he may please him who enlisted him as a soldier. And also if anyone competes in athletics, he is not crowned unless he competes according to the rules. But you be watchful in all things, endure afflictions, do the work of an evangelist, fulfil your ministry (2 Tim. 2:3-5; 4:5).

I have fought a good fight, I have finished my course, I have kept the faith: Henceforth there is laid up for me a crown of righteousness, which the Lord, the righteous judge, shall give me at that day: and not to me only, but unto all them also that love his appearing (2 Tim. 4:7-8).

Let us pray.

O Lord God our Father, You desire us to be in Your kingdom (Luke 12:32), but without obedience to Your Spirit, we will disappoint ourselves. Dear Father, guide our choices that we shall abound in grace and be faithful to You, regardless of our circumstances, and at last be with You in heaven, in the name of Jesus Christ, our Lord. Amen. We are grateful to You, Father, for granting our request.

Remain favored by God and man (Prov. 3:3-4).

Share with me how this book has been a blessing to you by sending a mail to nonyeokoyecounselling@gmail.com.

With love from

Your sister and friend,

Dr. Nonye Okoye

How to Receive the Conqueror's Spirit

Believe in the Lord Jesus Christ, and you will be saved... (Acts 16:31).

Human beings are dead in their spirit because of sin. Someone who is dead lacks the capacity to function. A dead person does not perform his duty. You are alive and yet dead if you are not doing what God brought you into the world to do. Your first need is the miracle of life. No other person gives life to the dead spirit of man than Jesus, the Son of the living God (John 5:24-25; cf. 1 John 5:12). His shed blood paid for the sin of the entire world and anyone who believes in Him as the Son of God will receive forgiveness from God and grace to live a life of righteousness (John 1:29; Acts 8:37; Eph. 2:8-9).

*Kiss the **Son**, lest he be angry, and ye perish from the way, when his wrath is kindled but a little. Blessed are all they that put their **trust in him*** (Ps. 2:12).

If you are still living in sin, admit you are a sinner and give no excuses for your sins. With a sincere heart, look upon Jesus to save you from sin; consider all He suffered for you on the tree at Calvary (1 Pet. 2:24), believe in His Sonship and put your faith in Him to receive your salvation (John 3:16-17). Trust Him and pray the simple but powerful prayer below to receive salvation, and thank God for saving you [you can pray in your own words or dialect]. *For whoever shall call upon the name of the LORD shall be saved* (Rom. 10:13).

An example of a prayer of salvation

Oh God, I have sinned against You. Be merciful to me, a sinner.

I believe Jesus is the Son of God and the only way to salvation, that He died for my sins and resurrected for my justification (Rom. 3:24- 25). I submit my entire life to Jesus this day; make me and use me as You will. I will do whatever You ask me and go wherever You send me. Baptize me with the Holy Spirit and fire and equip me for the work You called me to do. I pray in the name of Jesus. Amen. God, I am grateful that

You have adopted me by Your Son, Jesus Christ, and enabled His life of righteousness in me.

My beloved friend, the blood of Jesus Christ has washed away your sins and God will not remember them again (Is. 43:25). You are now born again by the Spirit of God who dwells in you and bears witness with your spirit that you are a child of God (John 3:7-8; Rom. 8:16).

The Holy Spirit is your seal, your proof of redemption (John 1:12-13; Eph. 1:13). He will **teach** you all things, **remind** you all things, and **guide** you into all truth (John 14:26; 16:13). Listen to and obey Him; He will not mislead you (1 John 2:27; Rom. 8:14). Being born again is living in the supernatural. Henceforth, operate with the right of sonship - the power of the Holy Spirit (John 1:12).

With a joyful heart and a face full of smiles, I say to you, Welcome to God's family, where the love of Christ binds all the siblings. Your eternal life and faith journey begin now (1 John 5:11). I pray for your quick and healthy transformation as you learn about your new family - the Kingdom's principles and practices.

Christianity is primarily your relationship with Jesus Christ as your personal Savior and the Lord of your life. Cling to and focus on Him so that no one will **distract you** and you become **disappointed** (Heb. 12:2). **He alone** is the Bishop of your soul (1 Pet. 2:25).

Abbreviations

cf. – compare

v. – verse

vs. – verses

Old Testament

Gen. – Genesis

Ex. – Exodus

Lev. – Leviticus

Num. – Numbers

Deut. – Deuteronomy

Josh. – Joshua

Judg. – Judges

Sam. – Samuel

Kin. – Kings

Chr. – Chronicles

Neh. – Nehemiah

Esth. – Esther

Ps. – Psalms

Prov. – Proverbs

Eccl. – Ecclesiastes

Song – Songs of Solomon

Is. – Isaiah

Jer. – Jeremiah

Lam. – Lamentation

Ezek. – Ezekiel

Dan. – Daniel

Hab. – Habakkuk

Hag. – Haggai

Zeph. – Zephaniah

Zech. – Zechariah

New Testament

Matt. – Matthew

Rom. – Romans

Cor. – Corinthians

Gal. – Galatians

Eph. – Ephesians

Phil. – Philippians

Col. – Colossians

Thess. – Thessalonians

Tim. – Timothy

Heb. – Hebrews

Pet. – Peter

Rev. – Revelation

References

Assessment and Psychological Treatment of Sexually Abused Female Adolescents in the Lagos Metropolis, PhD Thesis by Okoye Nonye Charity (one of the best five theses submitted by the University of Lagos Postgraduate School of Studies to National Universities Commission at Abuja in 2006)

Okoye, N. (2011, April 9), *Friendship,* The Guardian, Saturday column

Okoye, N. (2011, April 16), *Saying 'no' without Feeling Guilty,* The Guardian, Saturday column

9 789787 968093